The Diet FIX

Praise for The Diet Fix

"There is quite simply no writer on nutrition and dietetics anywhere in the world whose opinion I value more than that of Zoë Harcombe. Here, finally, is the weight-loss advice that is effective because it is based on hard science and presented by someone who has been there, tried them all and found what actually works. And keeps on working. For decades. If you are still searching for that elusive lifestyle prescription that will work for you, rejoice. You have finally found it."

Professor Tim Noakes, A1 rated scientist and Emeritus Professor, author of over 750 scientific books and articles

----

"Zoë Harcombe provides an invaluable resource for understanding the mess that is today's nutrition and chronic disease research. Her ability to think critically and sceptically about the latest research makes her among the very few trustworthy sources of information and guidance on this vitally important topic."

Gary Taubes, science and health journalist, co-founder of the Nutrition Science Initiative (NuSI) and author of *Good Calories, Bad Calories* and *The Case Against Sugar*

"Zoë Harcombe has the rare ability to explain complex scientific issues in a language we can all understand. She will take you on a journey explaining why weight loss diets don't work, and how you can eat your way to better metabolic health. Most people who write books about diet either don't really understand the science, or don't understand food. Harcombe gets the science and knows food. *The Diet Fix* is a must read."

Dr Peter Brukner, specialist Sports Physician, previously Team Doctor for Liverpool FC, the Australian national cricket and Olympic Athletics teams

----

"The subjects of nutrition, obesity, dieting and weight loss have become a battlefield where the weapons of choice are prejudice, dogma and a bone-headed resistance to facts. In this book Zoë Harcombe lays out the myths that underpin the current stupidity and explains very clearly, what will actually work to help people lose weight, and, far more importantly, keep it off. It is not a life of denial and constant hunger. It is simple and straightforward. It works, I know it works, I have spoken to hundreds of people for whom it has worked."

Dr Malcolm Kendrick, GP, speaker and author of *The Great Cholesterol Con* and *Doctoring Data*

"There's a revolution taking place to overthrow decades of official advice about what a healthy diet is and how best to lose weight, debunking the wrong-headed belief that all you have to do is eat less and move more. Dr Harcombe knows all about the misery and self-loathing that such a pattern creates and which the book aims to put an end to. The first step is to stop dieting and start eating good, freshly cooked food; the next is to never again count a calorie."

Jerome Burne, medical health journalist

"*The Diet Fix* is an easy-to-read explanation of why calorie counting doesn't work and what can be done to fix it. Dr Harcombe shows once again a mastery of nutrition science and is able to translate that into simple steps to improve your health."

Dr Jason Fung, Canadian kidney specialist and author of *The Obesity Code* and *The Diabetes Code*

"This is the book to read when you have wanted to lose weight, failed, and not known why. So many have followed the advice of 'experts' and been made to feel guilty for failing. What if that advice was wrong? Zoë Harcombe invites you to understand the reasons behind that 'failed' advice and gives fresh insight into the emotional aspect of weight control. Her dietary advice is simple, succinct and workable. That's the first step to success. Arguably, it's the only first step."

Dr Gary Fettke, Orthopaedic Surgeon, Tasmania, Australia

"To date nutrition has been a set of erroneous beliefs based upon caloric formulas that have harmed our society as a whole. In this book Dr Harcombe separates fact from fiction and presents the science of nutrition as humans were designed to eat and drink. A must-read for anyone who wants to optimise their health and weight."

Dr Robert Cwyes, MD, PhD, specialist in weight management and Bariatric Surgery for adults and adolescents

----

"Dr Harcombe brings an unparalleled command of the scientific literature on nutrition, plus a sharp eye for detail and a thoroughly rigorous approach. If there is a fact to hunt down, Harcombe is a bloodhound on the trail. What's more, her writing is always witty and bright, managing to bring even statistics to life. If I aimed to lose weight, there is no book I'd trust more than *The Diet Fix*."

Nina Teicholz, investigative journalist and author of *The Big Fat Surprise*

DISCLAIMER

The content of this book is intended to inform, entertain and provoke your thinking. This is not intended as medical advice. It may, however, make you question current medical and nutritional advice. That's your choice. It's your life and health in your hands. Neither the author nor the publisher can be held responsible or liable for any loss or claim arising from the use, or misuse, of the content of this book.

Published in 2019 by Short Books,
Unit 316, ScreenWorks, 22 Highbury Grove,
London, N5 2ER

10 9 8 7 6 5 4 3 2 1

ISBN: 978-1-78072-376-1

Cover design by Two Associates
Photographs: Smith & Gilmour
Food Styling: Vicki Keppel-Compton

Printed at CPI Group (UK) Ltd, Croydon, CR0 4YY

A CIP record of this book is available from the British Library.

How to lose
weight and
keep it off...
One last time

The
Diet
FIX

DR ZOË HARCOMBE

"How many calories are you supposed to eat if you're on a diet?" Tom said.

"About a thousand. Well, I usually aim for a thousand and come in at about fifteen hundred," I said, realizing as I said it that the last bit wasn't strictly true.

"A thousand?" said Tom incredulously. "But I thought you needed two thousand just to survive. How many calories in a boiled egg?" said Tom.

"Seventy-five."

"Banana?"

"Large or small?"

"Small."

"Peeled?"

"Yes."

"Eighty," I said, confidently.

"Olive?"

"Black or green?"

"Black."

"Nine."

"Hobnob?"

"Eighty-one."

"Box of Milk Tray?"

"Ten thousand, eight hundred and ninety-six."

"How do you know all this?" said Tom.

I thought about it. "I just do."

– *Bridget Jones's Diary,* Helen Fielding[1]

For my brother, Adrian, whose strength and appetite for life is awe-inspiring.

Contents

Introduction

"I still have the check I wrote to my first diet doctor
– Baltimore, 1977. I was 23 years old, 148 pounds, a
size 8, and I thought I was fat. The doctor put me on
a 1,200-calorie regimen, and in less than two weeks
I had lost ten pounds (there's nothing like the first
time...). Two months later, I'd regained 12. Thus
began the cycle of discontent, the struggle
with my body. With myself."

Oprah Winfrey[2]

With that first step, Oprah joined the dieting brigade
– Beverly Hills, Atkins, Scarsdale, Cabbage Soup –
we know them all; we've done them all. Like so many
other dieters, she lost weight, felt terrific, vowed never
to regain but always did and so the vicious cycle took
hold.

A former Miss Black Tennessee, Oprah is 5'6" and
was a 135lb beauty queen. She recalled putting on weight

when she moved to Chicago.[3] If Oprah gained 10lb, or even 20lb, when she moved, surely all she needed to do was lose that weight once? Lose weight and keep it off; that's all we need to do. Just one time.

Yet Oprah lost and regained and lost and regained with each and every diet. At her heaviest she was 237lb and full of self-loathing. Each time she hit the target, she did a special show parading in her 'slim' jeans or whatever outfit made her look and feel sensational.

The biggest loser

Back in 2010, I met a TV producer who was working on diet programmes. She shared that one of the complete bafflements in the TV world was that *The Biggest Loser* was massive as a show in the US, but a complete non-starter in the UK. The show ran on Living TV in the UK in 2005 and 2006. It moved to ITV in 2009 (not even prime time), but didn't last beyond 2012. The US show, in contrast, started in 2004 and ran for 17 seasons. The factoids on the show alone are extraordinary. The fastest 100lb loss took just six weeks!

The Biggest Loser became the subject of academic interest when a paper was published in May 2016.[4] The research team followed 14 of the 16 Season 8 contestants to see what happened after that sensational 'reveal' before and after moment.

Danny Cahill was the winner of Season 8. He dropped from 430lb to 191lb – a loss of 239lb in seven months. That's going from 30 stone 10lb to 13 stone 9lb in UK terminology and a loss of 108kg from 195 to 87kg for those in metric. That's immense by any standards.

The trouble is, *The Biggest Loser* contestants find that they cannot sustain the loss. They appear on the show looking a million dollars and the winner gets a quarter of a million dollars. But underneath it all, they don't feel a million dollars.

For one, they are barely able to stand through dehydration for the final weigh-in. They don't drink in the hours before and have saunas or wear sweat suits to drop every pound of fluid possible. Secondly, they have rolls of skin hanging off them as a result of the rapid weight loss. Danny explained that they 'dress carefully' and wear compression undergarments to hold everything in.

There will be immediate weight gain as soon as contestants have a glass of water. Indeed, the first few glasses of water will be retained just to normalise body fluids. This is weight, not fat, but it doesn't take long for the fat to also return. Danny started a motivational speaking tour after winning the show, but only managed to keep his weight below 255lb (18 stone 3lb/116kg) by exercising for several hours a day.

Despite his best efforts, Danny could not maintain his

loss and he has regained more than 100lb. He's not alone. Most of the contestants he beat have regained much, if not all, of the weight that they sweated so brutally to lose. Some are even heavier than when they started the show.[5]

My story

I know how Oprah, Danny and others feel. I've not been as heavy as Danny and I've not lost as many pounds as Oprah, but I have been on a calorie deficit diet – many times. The first time, I lost weight, regained it and a bit more. Then I went on another calorie-controlled diet, lost weight (not as easily the second time round) regained it and a bit more. And then another, and another.

When I started this vicious cycle aged 15, I was 5'2" and about 120lb. That's a body mass index (BMI) bang in the middle of the normal range, but a couple of comments at school and I thought I was fat. I went to a newsagent and picked up a booklet about calorie counting.

The book said, "To lose 1lb of fat you need to create a deficit of 3,500 calories." That was supposedly it – the secret to weight loss. Apparently all I needed to do was eat less and/or do more, and for every 3,500 fewer calories eaten and/or 3,500 more calories exercised off, I would magically lose 1lb of body fat. The timescale was supposed to be completely flexible too – cut back by 500 calories a day to lose 1lb in seven days. Or cut back by 1,000 calories a day to lose 2lb per week. I've seen suggestions that cutting back by a 50-calorie biscuit a day will result in a 5lb weight loss at the end of the year.

As Blackadder might have said: "This is wronger than a very wrong thing!" We'll show this belief to be completely false in Chapter 1.

My mother was a sports teacher, so I was already following in her footsteps and 'doing more' than any of my peers: swimming, hockey, rounders, tennis, badminton, athletics – you name it – I was doing more of it. The food bit seemed like a piece of cake (excuse the pun). I went on to do maths and economics at Cambridge University, so memorising the calorie content of many foods and totting them up every time I ate was a doddle.

I started my 1,000-calorie-a-day diet in the autumn and began to lose weight. By spring, when winter tracksuits came off, my sports team-mates noticed my weight loss. In the six months of dieting, according to the 3,500-calorie formula in my diet book, I should have lost 52lb in fat alone, and more on top in terms of water and muscle (sadly) – approximately 60lb, in fact. I had lost a fraction of that. I'd gone under 100lb, but had lost a third of what the formula said I should have done.

I cut back even more. I reached the point over the

summer where I was trying to live on black coffee and green apples – approximately 400 calories a day. At my lowest weight, I dipped under 90lb and I started getting threatened with school/doctor interventions. So I decided that I would stick at that weight for a while, take the pressure off, and then return as soon as possible to what by now had become an obsession. Only that didn't work out too well.

The booklet said that weight could be maintained at approximately 1,500 calories a day. I hadn't spotted that bit when I started my first diet. I hadn't seen 'the small print' when I was excited about 'the new me'. I hadn't signed up to eating three quarters of what I needed to eat (and a fraction of what I had eaten as a sporty teenager) for the rest of my life. It turned out that this too was a lie. If only one could eat three quarters of calories needed and not regain weight.

I started on my 1,500-calorie-a-day 'maintenance' diet and I started to regain faster than Usain Bolt can sprint. I panicked and tried to slash back to the apples and black coffee. Only I didn't seem to have the willpower for that any more. I had reacquainted myself with the taste of cereal, toast and calorie-counted 'fake food' and I wanted more of it. The more I tried to cut back, the more food seemed to compel me to eat it. I was at the start of the worst period of my life.

My late teens and what should have been the best of times – the privilege of attending one of the finest universities in the world – were marred by being in complete turmoil about food. I went from 90lb to closer to 140lb, but even the despised extra weight wasn't as bad as the sense of being powerless. I was a drug addict, desperate to get my fix, but knowing that I would feel so much better if I could get my starving/bingeing under control.

Food is, in many ways, the worst addiction to have. We can give up cigarettes, we can avoid alcohol, and we can come off social media. We can't stop consuming things. (The temporary success of liquid diets, by the way, is largely due to the fact that they stop us eating for a period of time.)

My story has a happy ending. Indeed, I've been enjoying the happy ending for over 20 years. I've found a way to maintain my ideal weight (110lb/50kg) without hunger, starvation or deprivation. I enjoy food in a way that I could never have imagined. I used the trauma of the 'worst period of my life' to start a long-term study of obesity, weight loss and emotional relationships with food.

It has been a fascinating journey and I have been helping others to get slim and stay slim since 2004. I want to share the findings with you in this book. I want to help you to get off the Oprah rollercoaster of losing, regaining and probably a bit more. I want the next pounds/kilos that you lose to be the last that you need to lose – the ones that come off and stay off. I want this for you because I know from academic research the deep anxiety that people feel about regaining lost weight – of becoming obese after having tasted what slim feels like...

Florida study

A measure of the relative distress that people feel about their weight can be made by offering a forced choice of options. A shocking study was undertaken at the University of Florida in 1991.[6] The researchers questioned 47 patients (39 women and eight men), who had lost weight after bariatric surgery and who had maintained a weight loss of at least 43kg (95lb) for at least three years.

The patients were asked seven forced-choice questions: Would you rather be morbidly obese for life or be normal weight for life and one of the following for life: i) deaf; ii) have very bad acne; iii) have heart disease; iv) be unable to read; v) be an insulin-dependent diabetic; vi) be blind; vii) have one leg amputated.

Every single patient said that they would rather be deaf, have very bad acne, have heart disease, be unable to read, be an insulin-dependent diabetic, and normal weight for life, than be morbidly obese with none of those conditions. Forty-two out of 47 patients said that they would rather be blind and normal weight than morbidly obese for life. Forty-three out of 47 patients gave being normal weight and having one leg amputated as a preferred option to morbid obesity.

This is one of the most staggering pieces of obesity research that I have ever come across. If anyone ever doubts how much we want to be slim, this is the paper to show them. Having experienced obesity, we would rather be blind, deaf or have a leg amputated than be obese again. That is the extent of our desire to be slim and yet two thirds of people in the UK, USA and Australia are overweight and one quarter obese. Why?

Why?

My research has led to the conclusion that our public health advice has more likely caused the obesity epidemic than helped it. We are constantly being told that we need to eat less/do more. That's insulting for starters. It's effectively saying that we are greedy (we eat too much) and lazy (we do too little). As well as being judgemental, it's just not helpful.

The people who gave this advice can't have seen the evidence from the past hundred years showing that it simply doesn't work. I'll share the key, fascinating studies with you in Chapter 2. Nor have diet advisors worked out *why* 'eat less/do more' doesn't work. I'll share that with you in Chapter 3. We'll see how trying to cut calories drives us into a spiral of continually trying to maintain an unsustainable deficit to avoid regain.

Does this resonate with you? Can you empathise with

Oprah and Danny and millions more dieters across the world? Have you lost weight, felt great and vowed never to go back to the old you? Did the weight come back despite every single thing that you tried in desperation? Maybe you ended up even heavier than when you started and absolutely devastated that your good intentions came to nothing?

You are not alone. We have been fed many cruel lies when it comes to weight loss. We want to be slim more than pretty much anything else in the world. It's not our fault that we're not. We are not failures – the slimming advice that we have been given has set us up to fail.

Did you know that there is no evidence for that 3,500-calorie promise in diet books? Did you know that there is no evidence that calorie deficit diets have ever achieved long-term, sustained weight loss? Do you know what happens when you try to eat less and/or do more? Would you like to know why calorie deficit diets don't work? Would you like to know what does work?

Excellent, let's go!

Just one other thing – we are going to need to talk about our emotional relationship with food. I can get you to the point where you can lose weight without hunger, but so many of us eat without hunger already. We eat because we're bored. We eat because we're angry. We eat because friends or family have wound us up. We eat because someone at work was mean to us. We eat because we think it will cheer us up. We need to sort out all of this too, because it's getting in the way of us being that slim person that we so want to be.

PART I

No more calorie counting

1
The calorie myth

"To lose 1lb of fat you need to create a
deficit of 3,500 calories."

The British Dietetic Association[7]

If the above quotation were true, I'd be dead! I'd have died within a year of starting that 1,000-calorie-a-day diet; the one that became the 400-calorie-a-day diet. However few calories I was eating, I maintained at least close to, if not beyond, a 1,000-calorie deficit each day. I should have lost 104lb in fat alone in the first year – more on top from water and lean tissue. I should, therefore, have lost my entire body weight – 120lb. I would, of course, have ceased to exist some time before I became weightless.

People laugh when I say at conferences: "I weigh 110lb. If the calorie theory worked, I'd be 6lb in a year's time!" They're still laughing when I clarify: "Actually, the calorie theory is only about fat. I'd lose more in muscle and water and so I'd be minus a few pounds."

I then ask them why they're laughing. This is the promise that people are still reading in magazines, online and in public health documents. People start a diet on a Monday morning precisely because they think their deprivation will be rewarded with weight loss each and every week. People go to slimming clubs each and every week. Confident that they've stuck perfectly to the regime, they're expecting a good result and they jump on the scales and they're gutted. Yet another week of no reward for the punishment that they have endured. Is it any wonder that people give up and eat whatever they like?

Every one of these slimmers could work out that the calorie theory is a myth. I'm kicking myself for not working it out when I was 16. It is being proven wrong worldwide on a daily basis and yet it is still published as if true in official and popular literature across the globe. It's time for the fact that the calorie theory is a myth to go mainstream...

Where did the calorie myth come from?

I also ask people in conference lectures if they know where the calorie theory comes from. They look blank, so I tell them: "Don't worry – nor do I!" I also tell them that they're not alone – none of the powers-that-be have any clue either.

I am still trying to find the earliest reference to the

3,500 formula and to trace it through to when it became 'folklore'. While researching, I came across a book called *Diet and Health* by Lulu Hunt Peters (1918).[8] Lulu stated: "Five hundred Calories equal approximately 2 ounces of fat. Two ounces per day would be about 4 pounds per month, or 48 pounds per year. Cutting out 1000 Calories per day would equal a reduction of approximately 8 pounds per month, or 96 pounds per year." That's the formula – nicely set out in 1918.

An article from the *Chicago Daily Tribune* in 1959 contained the line: "a pound of fat is lost whenever the body burns up 3,500 calories by diet or exercise".[9] The way that this was asserted suggested that it was already a well-known 'fact' by this date, but did Lulu start it or perpetuate it?

A couple of extracts in *Diet and Health* make me think that it is entirely plausible that Lulu did effectively originate "The Calorie Formula":

1. On the opening page, Lulu talks about the words in her book and says: "They are clever. *I wrote them myself.*" (Lulu's own emphasis in italics). I don't think that Lulu was being arrogant. I think that she was telling us that this was her original thinking.
2. Chapter 2 of Lulu's book was called "Key to the calories" and there was a note explaining how to pronounce calories [Pronounced Kal'-o-ri]. This tells us that calories were so little known at the time

that people needed to be told how to pronounce the word.

If only we had stayed so blissfully ignorant about calories, or at least had come to see them as fuel for the body – which is all that they are.

If Lulu had the right to be proud of her 'cleverness' and if she really did break something revolutionary to the women of Los Angeles in 1918, we may indeed have one woman to thank for "The Calorie Formula", which is the foundation of weight loss advice to date. If anyone knows of a reference earlier than 1918, I would be interested for the sake of research, but it actually matters less where it originated and more that it has held as fact for at least 100 years and yet cannot be proven.

Where do public health bodies think the calorie myth comes from?

In 2009 I had a thought: if I don't know where this calorie theory comes from, why not ask the people who use it? I thought that seven particular organisations in the UK should know the origin. I thus approached:

- The British Dietetic Association
- Dietitians in Obesity Management
- The National Health Service

- The National Institute for Clinical Excellence (as it was then – it's now the National Institute for Care and Health Excellence)
- The Department of Health
- The National Obesity Forum
- The Association for the Study of Obesity

I first asked the British Dietetic Association (BDA). They didn't even attempt to answer the question. They suggested that I ask a dietician, which amused me because they are the body representing all dieticians. I happened to be at an obesity conference soon after receiving this reply, so I asked several dieticians and no one knew where the 3,500 calorie formula came from. One dietician said to me: "You've made us think how much we were just 'told' during our training, with no explanation. A group of us over there don't even know where 'five-a-day' comes from." Well, that's a myth too, so things weren't looking good for the calorie theory at this stage!

After this, I contacted the other six organisations. One after the other, they all failed to answer my question:

I am an obesity researcher and I am trying to find out the rationale behind the statement: 'One pound of fat contains 3,500 calories, so to lose 1lb a week you need a deficit of 500 calories a day.' This specific reference is a verbatim quotation from the British Dietetic Association's (BDA) weight loss leaflet *Want to*

Lose Weight and Keep it Off? The BDA reply was 'we do not hold information on the topic'. As this formula is the foundation of all current weight loss advice, it is critical to be able to prove it. Please can you let me know where this formula comes from and the evidence for it?

The NHS answered: "Unfortunately our Lifestyles team do not hold this information and are unable to assist you with your enquiry. I would suggest you contact the DOH to see if they can help."

I forwarded the query and the NHS response to the Department of Health. Meanwhile, I wrote to the other organisations in tandem. The National Obesity Forum replied and advised me to contact the Association for the Study of Obesity (ASO). I thanked the NOF for their reply but pointed out that their own website quoted the 3,500 formula verbatim and also had the following classic use of the formula: "one less (sic) 50 calorie plain biscuit per day could help you lose 5lb (2.3kg) in a year – and one extra biscuit means you could gain that in a year!"

The National Institute for Care and Health Excellence (NICE) is the organisation in the UK responsible for issuing evidence-based guidelines. Their reply was priceless: "Whilst our guidance does contain reference to studies involving 500 calorie deficit diets we do not hold any information about the rationale behind the statement 'one pound of fat contains 3,500 calories, so to lose 1lb a week you need a deficit of 500 calories a day.'" i.e. although we are an evidence-based organisation, we have no evidence.

Dieticians in Obesity Management (DOM) and ASO were the most helpful by far. Alas, both still completely failed to prove the 3,500 formula. Both organisations sent me back details of the same study. The study was from a NICE document, so it was amusing that NICE didn't seem to be aware of this.

The NICE document, *Management of Obesity: Full Guidance* (December 2006), contained one particular study that was being offered as evidence for the calorie theory. In Table 15.14 of this long document, there were details of an experiment involving 12 people. They were put on a diet that created a deficit of 600 calories a day and they were compared with people who didn't go on a diet. After 12 months, the 12 dieters varied between being 7.8kg lighter and 0.4kg heavier. On average, after a year, they were about 5kg (11lb) lighter than people doing nothing.

The calorie formula says that these 12 people should each have lost 600 x 365/3,500 = 62.6lb of fat. Not an ounce (of fat) more or less. AND, there should have been no range of results – everyone should have lost exactly the same (that's what happens with a mathematical formula). The least anyone lost (let's put it all into pounds) was 0.8lb and the most anyone lost was 17.2lb. Even the highest weight loss was 45lb lower than it should have been. This is also all about fat – we haven't even started looking at muscle or water loss. And it's a study of just 12 people. There are 1.1 billion overweight people in the world and we can't prove a formula using 12 of them.

DOM presented the same study as: "There is good evidence that this level of deficit [600 calories a day] produces weight differences of approx 5kg at 1 year." DOM, key proponents of the calorie formula, acknowledged that one year of a 600-calorie-a-day deficit might produce a weight loss of approximately 11lb – i.e. significantly less than the 62.6lb that should be lost as fat alone according to the formula.

The organisations approached have all spectacularly failed to answer where the 3,500 theory comes from, let alone provide any evidence of its validity.

The small print

I bet that the 12 people who went on that 600-calorie-a-day deficit diet weren't told that they would need to keep up a deficit for life or otherwise face regaining the weight. It's bad enough that the calorie theory is a myth. It's bad enough that you won't lose the amount of weight that you expect. It's even worse that you will lower your metabolism such that you need to continue to eat substantially less merely to avoid regain.

A study in the *Lancet* in December 2017, known as

the DiRECT study,[10] missed out the small print. The study was about putting type 2 diabetes into remission by using a very low-calorie diet to achieve weight loss. The toughest part of the diet involved three to five months of consuming 800 calories in the form of liquid meal replacements. The participants were then supposed to try to maintain the weight loss. The article was vague as to how this would be achieved so I entered into correspondence with the study authors. It turned out that calorie intake needed to be maintained long term at no more than two thirds of what the pre-diet intake had been. The missing small print for this diet was "once you start on the calorie deficit, you need to maintain it". I don't hold out long-term hope for this method of reversing type 2 diabetes.

As we will see in the next chapter, even when people have been monitored 24-7 during calorie deficit experiments, they have found the hunger intolerable and they have lost a fraction of the weight that they were expected to lose. In the next chapter, we will take a look at one of the most famous dieting experiments ever undertaken. It was done in the 1940s, during the Second World War. Food is much more widely available today than it was back then and so prolonged calorie restriction is even more difficult.

Maybe Victoria Beckham has mastered deprivation for life. Maybe Wallace Simpson did (she who is said to have coined the statement "you can never be too rich or too thin"). Monks seem to do pretty well with denial too. As for us lesser mortals – we just can't seem to function, let alone be happy and high performing, when we don't have enough petrol in the tank.

Fear not – there's a wonderful way out of this 'eat less, need less, can't keep it up, regain' nightmare. We'll get to it soon enough. I'm betting that you've been conditioned to believe that weight is all about calories for a very long time. It's going to take another chapter or two before you're prepared to ditch 'eat less/do more' for ever – which is what you must do to start losing weight and keep it off.

2
The evidence against low-calorie diets

"98% of diets fail."

Anon

"Most obese persons will not stay in treatment for obesity. Of those who stay in treatment, most will not lose weight, and of those who do lose weight, most will regain it."

Stunkard and McLaren-Hume (1959)[11]

The Minnesota Starvation Experiment

The bombing of Pearl Harbour brought the Americans into the Second World War on 8th December 1941. Europe had been at war since September 1939. Fuel rationing started in the UK later that year and food rationing started in January 1940.

As Europe continued to be decimated and the future impact on America remained unknown, an American doctor, Ancel Keys, realised that it would be crucial to find out what would happen if the war did not end soon and rationing turned to starvation. He set about one of the most ambitious health experiments ever undertaken – to provide the definitive study of hunger and re-feeding. Keys achieved this goal and also, unintentionally, he provided one of the most important insights into dieting and weight loss to this day.

The Minnesota Starvation Experiment started with an advert, posted across America in May 1944: "Will you starve that they be better fed?" Two hundred conscientious objectors volunteered, as an alternative to war, and Keys and his team of researchers whittled these down to 36 men. The men (all aged 20-33) were chosen for their physical and mental resilience. The results, 1,385 pages in total, were published in 1950 in *The Biology of Human Starvation.*[12]

The experiment was referred to by the men as "C.P.S." This stood for "Civilian Public Service", which was the collective term for programmes for US conscientious objectors during the war.

The one-year experiment was split into four phases:

- **The Control Period (12 weeks).** The first few weeks of the experiment were used to work out the daily calorie requirement for the men. It was established that the men maintained their weight at approximately 3,210 calories a day while walking 22 miles each week. That's an average of three miles a day (45-60 minutes walking).

- **The Starvation Period (24 weeks).** The fact that the study was referred to as a "starvation experiment" is interesting, because the six-month 'starvation' period was actually a calorie-controlled diet of approximately 1,600 calories per day with 45-60 minutes walking per day. That's pretty generous by the standards of today's diets. The meals were made up of foods typically available in Europe during the latter stages of the war: potatoes, turnips, bread and macaroni; i.e. starchy carbohydrates – the foods that we are advised to base our meals on. Keys set out to achieve a 25% weight loss in each man in 24 weeks.

- **The Restricted Rehabilitation Period (12 weeks).** The men were divided into four groups of eight (four had been dismissed for stealing food and bingeing). They were given different calorie, protein and vitamin intakes to see what would best re-nourish them back to health.

- **The Unrestricted Rehabilitation Period (8 weeks).** For the final period, the men could eat as much as they wanted and the research team carefully recorded what they did in fact eat.

This amazing study tells us the following four things about dieting and weight loss:

1. Hunger is comparable with war in terms of the devastating effect it has on people.

Many of the volunteers came to believe that going to war would have been an easier option than sticking to the diet.

The men were required to keep diaries during the experiment. One man, called Sam Legg, recorded: "I have been more depressed than ever in my life… I thought that there was only one thing that would pull me out of the doldrums, that is release from C.P.S. I decided to get rid of some fingers. Ten days ago, I jacked up my car and let the car fall on these fingers. It was premeditated." A few days later, Sam cut three fingers off his left hand while chopping wood. When he was asked why he did this, Sam couldn't explain. He didn't know if it had been deliberate self-harm, maybe in an attempt to overcome the pain of starvation, or whether he was just too hungry to perform normal tasks.

Sam was an extreme case, but all the physically and mentally healthy men, put on a calorie-controlled diet, were turned into physical and emotional shadows of their former selves in a matter of weeks.

Physically, the men reported incessant hunger, weakness and exhaustion, and they lost 21% of their strength in the first 12 weeks alone. They experienced dizziness, muscle wasting, hair loss and reduced coordination.

The experiment took place at the University of Minnesota, giving the men unlimited opportunity to study anything they wished. It could be argued that they were removed from their normal routine and were thus more likely to become preoccupied with food. However, they could have whiled away the experiment reading and learning. Instead, within weeks, the men withdrew from their classes because they simply didn't have the energy or motivation to attend. They had libraries of literature to fascinate them and yet there was only one thing on their minds: food.

Psychologically, the men became obsessed with food, meal times and everything to do with eating. The study documented, "For some, the fascination was so great that they actually changed occupations after the experiment; three became chefs, and one went into agriculture." They had to 'buddy up' to avoid breaking their diets, as their drive to binge was so enormous. Before the buddy system was put in place, a couple did get hold of some forbidden food and binge, and suffered extreme guilt and self-loathing as a result. (It is fair to assume, therefore, that, had the men not been confined during the experiment, all of them would have given up on their diet.) The men reported extreme depression, irritability and a sense of deprivation, and they lost all interest in sex. They actually lost all interest in anything other than food – such is the human drive to overcome hunger.

2. The calorie promise – "To lose one pound of fat you need to create a deficit of 3,500 calories" – is a myth.

We saw this in the previous chapter, but the Minnesota Starvation Experiment proved this statement to be false even by 1950. The first diet book that I read should never have been written.

If the 3,500 formula were correct, during the 24 weeks, every man should have lost at least 78lb in fat alone and more on top of this in water and lean tissue. The men's average weight loss was less than half of this – 37lb.

If the 3,500 formula were correct, the lightest man in the study, Bob Villwock from Ohio, should have finished the study below 3 stone (he would, of course, have died long before this).

If the 3,500 formula were correct, all the men should have lost exactly the same weight with the same deficit. Each man lost a different amount. This landmark study showed the calorie theory to be a myth and its publication in 1950 should have ended the use of this statement from that point on.

3. The less you eat, the less you must continue to eat to have any chance of losing more weight. Weight loss will stop, at some point, whether you like it or not.

The men started the diet consuming approximately 1,600 calories a day, but Keys soon found that he needed to lower the calorie intake repeatedly to try to keep the goal weight loss on track. The weight loss slowed so much that some men were only allowed 1,000 calories a day. All the men reached a plateau around week 20 and further weight loss could not be achieved. At least one diary recorded weight gain in the final month of "The Starvation Period".

4. The body will do whatever it takes to reverse the effects of starvation/dieting.
Remember that this study was about the risk of food running out during the war and the need to understand what harm that could cause. The purpose of the final two rehabilitation periods was to see how quickly people could be brought back to full health if war ended and food became available once more.

During "The Restricted Rehabilitation Period", the four different groups of men were given 400, 800, 1,200 or 1,600 extra calories per day. Within each group of eight men, some were also given vitamin and protein supplements. Keys wanted to see what best helped recovery. He concluded that the only thing that determined the speed at which the men recovered was the calorie intake. The body didn't respond to vitamins or protein – it just wanted the calorie deficit to be reversed.

You won't be surprised to learn, therefore, that when the men were given free access to food, in the final two months, they overate and binged like crazy. One man managed to eat 11,500 calories in one day. The men still felt hungry consuming twice the number of calories that had maintained their weight in the control period. The researchers noted in the study: "Subject No. 20 stuffs himself until he is bursting at the seams, to the point of being nearly sick and still feels hungry"; "No. 1 ate until he was uncomfortably full"; and subject "No. 30 had so little control over the mechanics of 'piling it in' that he simply had to stay away from food because he could not find a point of satiation even when he was 'full to the gills'."

The participants not only gained all their weight back but ended up weighing approximately 10% more than before the experiment. Men who had previously shown no awareness of body size and image reported 'feeling fat'.

This study proved that calorie deficit dieting doesn't work. We can't sustain hunger. We become obsessed with food. We end up needing to consume fewer and fewer calories to avoid regain. This would require us to stay hungry long term. We can't manage a 1,000-1,600-calorie-a-day diet for 24 weeks even when we're guarded 24-7, have all meals prepared for us and think that we're participating in a vital study to help our country at war. What hope have we got when we try to start a calorie-controlled diet in the real world and the sandwich trolley arrives at 11am?!

What's more this is not only about individuals. Surely we have also just observed the prerequisite for a global obesity epidemic? Eat less, get hungry, slow the metabolism, increase the desire to eat, reduce the desire to move, gain weight, try to eat less again and so on. We have certainly just described the western world, since we started our obsession with calorie counting.

Francis Benedict

While undoubtedly the best study, the Minnesota Starvation Experiment wasn't the first. My research suggests that the first study was undertaken by a brilliant American man called Francis G. Benedict.[13] Benedict had studied at Harvard University and was a qualified chemist, physiologist and nutritionist. He was perfectly qualified to do the work that he undertook on calories, human metabolism and basal metabolic rate.* Much of his work still stands today.

In 1917, Benedict was curious to see how calorie restriction affected our metabolism. He put 12 young men on a calorie deficit diet. The goal was to achieve a 10% weight loss and to see what happened to the metabolism as a result. Benedict wondered if a 10% weight loss would result in a 10% reduction in metabolism.

The 12 men averaged 3,100 calories per day before the diet. During the diet, they averaged between 1,700 and 2,400 calories per day, so this was no starvation diet. In just over four months, an average loss of 10.6% of body

---

* Basal Metabolic Rate (BMR) equates to the number of calories that you need even if you do nothing all day – lying sick in bed, for example.

weight was achieved by the group of 12 men. The men reported hunger and extreme cold. Their metabolism and energy expenditure dropped so dramatically that, if they consumed more than 2,000 calories a day, they regained weight. The precise reduction in calories required to avoid regain was 37%; more than one third. The 10% weight loss had resulted in a 37% drop in energy needed.

When allowed to eat as they wished, the men regained all the weight lost within a fortnight. Barely a couple more weeks later, the men were, on average, 3kg (6.6lb) above their initial weight. Only one of the 12 men ended up at a lower weight than before the diet. Two ended up approximately 7kg (15lb) heavier than when they started the experiment.

Stunkard and McLaren-Hume

Dr Albert Stunkard was an American psychiatrist who founded the Centre for Weight and Eating Disorders. He was fascinated by obesity and won many awards for his work during his long career. He collaborated with a dietician called Mavis McLaren-Hume on his most cited article, which was written in 1959.[14] McLaren-Hume worked at the nutrition clinic of the New York Hospital, which gave her unique access to obese patients and their medical records. Having reviewed the literature from the first half of the 20th century and having done their own study at the New York clinic, Stunkard and McLaren-Hume concluded: "Most obese persons will not stay in treatment for obesity. Of those who stay in treatment, most will not lose weight, and of those who do lose weight, most will regain it."

Stunkard and McLaren-Hume's own study showed that only 12% of obese patients lost 20lb, despite having stones to lose; only one person in 100 lost 40lb; and, two years later, only 2% of patients had maintained a 20lb weight loss.

I think that this could be where the often-quoted "98% of diets fail" comes from.

Marion Franz

One of my favourite studies was undertaken by a group of American researchers. Marion Franz and seven colleagues performed something called a systematic review of weight loss studies.[15] This means that they looked at all weight loss studies that met their chosen criteria and reviewed them together. This is far more powerful than looking at just one study. Their criteria were gold standard too. They only looked at what we call 'randomised controlled trials'. This is where an intervention happens in one group and the outcome is compared with a control group where nothing happened, so that we can see the direct impact of the intervention – in this case a diet of some kind. They also only looked at studies with at least a one-year follow-up. Any studies that lasted just a few weeks, or even months, were excluded.

They ended up with 80 weight loss studies in their systematic review, which was published in 2007. The studies were all from the period between January 1997 and September 2004. A total of 26,455 participants were involved in the 80 studies. At the one-year follow-up, across all the studies, 29% of people had dropped out and were no longer available for assessment. That was the first interesting finding – as with the Minnesota Starvation Experiment, people struggled to stick to a diet even when they knew they were involved in an important academic study. Many of these diets were not tough either – some just involved doing some exercise or even taking a weight loss drug.

The researchers grouped the diets into eight categories: advice alone; exercise alone; diet alone; meal replacements; diet and exercise; very low-calorie (liquid) diets; orlistat and sibutramine.

The latter two were drug interventions. Orlistat (Alli) is a drug that impairs absorption of fat. It has a number of rather disastrous side effects including wind, diarrhoea and anal leakage. I kid you not! When the pill first became available in the US, the manufacturer, GlaxoSmithKline, advised that first-timers should wear dark trousers and/or carry a change of clothes just in case they experienced the embarrassment of 'pooping their pants'. (If anyone ever doubts how desperate we all are to be slim – remember what we are prepared to risk in the pursuit of weight loss!)

Sibutramine was traded as Reductil (among other names). I say "was" because it was withdrawn under a European Medicines Agency directive in January 2010 after a study showed there to be a risk of serious cardiovascular events from taking the drug. The drug only achieved modest weight loss anyway – 2-4kg more than with the placebo – and this was not thought to be worth the risk.

The Franz review contained some very interesting findings:

- The smallest weight loss was achieved in the studies where the intervention was exercise alone. The adage 'you can't outrun a bad diet' was nicely proven by this study.
- The largest weight loss was achieved in the very low-calorie (liquid) diets. You know the ones – LighterLife, Cambridge Diet, etc – the liquid shakes made up of mostly skimmed milk and sugar and added vitamins and minerals (because there's naff-all nutrition in the product without adding these).
- The largest weight loss group was also the largest weight regain group. The very low-calorie (liquid) diet studies grouped together dipped to the lowest point and then the regain was almost as rapid.

- Something happened at approximately six months. In every group, weight loss was lowest at the half-year mark and then regain started. This is remarkably consistent with the Minnesota Starvation Experiment, in which weight loss was virtually impossible to achieve at 24 weeks. It is as if our bodies might tolerate an energy deficit for about six months, but no longer than this.
- The main conclusion from the authors of the Franz review was: "A mean weight loss of 5 to 8.5kg was observed during the first 6 months from interventions involving a reduced-energy diet and/or weight loss medications with weight plateaus at approximately 6 months. In studies extending to 48 months, a mean 3 to 6kg of weight loss was maintained with none of the groups experiencing weight regain to baseline."

Despite some of the interventions achieving far greater than a 1,000-calorie-a-day deficit, the average weight loss was 11-19lb in six months. The "plateau at approximately six months" was better described as the bottom of the weight loss curve before regain started. After four years, where data were available, dieters were lucky to be 3-6kg (6-13lb) down from their starting weight. Does that sound like a good deal? If you can stick to a diet – whether diet and exercise, or a drug intervention, or liquid meal replacement/food avoidance – for four years, you might be a few pounds down at the end of your ordeal.

I first saw this graph presented by Professor Nick Finer at the Wales National Obesity Forum conference in May 2010. His pessimistic, but realistic, conclusion was that such interventions would at best set weight gain back a few years. The Franz study used an 'advice alone' group as a baseline – suggesting that people who just received healthy eating advice, but did nothing to change their behaviour, would stay at the same weight. Professor Finer questioned whether this was a fair comparison. He thought that the average person would gain weight over time if they made no attempt to lose it. Finer wondered whether calorie deficit diets would be needed not to achieve weight loss, but simply to delay inevitable weight gain.

No wonder that the professional obesity world has all but given up on adults and is trying to prevent childhood obesity instead. (Dear reader, please don't despair at this stage – there is an alternative to starving to stand still. In fact, rejoice because you never need to starve to lose weight again.)

At the time the studies in the Franz review were being undertaken, US adults alone were spending more than $50 billion per year on weight loss efforts.[16] The expectations were well noted in the Franz article: women participating in a weight loss programme reported their goal as an average 32% reduction in body weight. The actual results quantified by Franz were closer to one tenth of this (3%). Then there was the plateau and subsequent regain at six months; therefore maintenance became the next challenge.

The article reported: "Health care professionals and participants often express frustration believing that if a reduced energy intake is maintained (or decreased even further as was done in some studies), weight loss should continue. This appears not to happen... (and) ...if weight-loss interventions are discontinued, weight regain is likely to occur."

How many dieters know that these are the facts for 'eat less/do more' weight loss interventions? The expectations of dieters are not unreasonable. Dieters have been promised substantial weight loss by the 3,500-calorie formula.

In my experience of working with people desperate to lose weight, 2lb a week is the minimum they expect to lose. One woman said to me: "With nearly half my current weight to lose, I can't cope with 2lb a week." Why was I the first person to be honest and tell this 60-year-old that, if she lost 2lb a week, week in week out (in fat alone) until she reached her target weight, she would be the first person in the world ever to do so.

The healthy low-fat vs. healthy low-carb study

Almost 100 years after the Benedict study, we had another study disproving the calorie theory, although that

47

was not the intention of the trial.

The study was led by a researcher from Stanford University, Professor Christopher Gardner.[17] It involved 609 adults aged 18 to 50 with a BMI between 28 and 40. The participants were randomly assigned to either a healthy low-fat (HLF) diet or a healthy low-carb (HLC) diet. The main aim of this study was to prioritise healthy food, whether or not that healthy food was low-fat or low-carb.

The study was one year long and, during that time, the groups averaged calorie deficits of approximately 184,000 for the HLF group and 210,000 for the HLC group. The 3,500-calorie formula would mean that the HLF group should have lost 53lb of fat and the HLC group, 60lb of fat (both should have lost many pounds more – approximately 15% more – in lean tissue and water). Both groups were also encouraged to undertake 150 minutes of moderately intensive aerobic physical activity per week, so the energy deficit would have been even greater than that measured by food intake. Consequently weight loss should have been even greater – and formulaic – according to the calorie theory. The actual weight loss, in both groups, was far less than this – 11lb (5.3kg) for the HLF diet and 13lb (6kg) for the HLC diet.

There was another really interesting finding in this study. The researchers started each group off at an extreme low-fat or low-carb diet and then allowed the dieters to move towards a fat or carb level that they individually found to be workable. The study started with the HLF

48

group instructed to limit their fat intake to 20g a day and the HLC group instructed to limit their carb intake to 20g a day. After 12 months, the low-fat group was averaging 57g of fat and the low-carb group was averaging 132g of carb. Both groups had moved substantially away from the extremes.

The 'chance of losing weight' article

Perhaps the final nail in the calorie theory coffin was hammered into place in July 2015. Newspapers worldwide ran headlines such as "The vast majority of people who pile on the pounds never lose them in the long run" and "'Slim chance' of returning to normal weight". The media interest came from a study, which was led by Dr Alison Fildes at King's College London and published in the *American Journal of Public Health*.[18]

The researchers took a sample of adults (20 years and older), from a UK database, between 2004 and 2014. They analysed data for 76,704 obese men and 99,791 obese women. They excluded anyone who had received bariatric surgery and then estimated the chance of the obese men and women studied attaining either normal weight or a 5% reduction in body weight.

These people were followed for up to nine years. During this time, 1,283 men and 2,245 women reached normal body weight. For men and women in the 30-34.9

BMI (obese) category at the start of the study, the chance of attaining normal weight in any one year was 1 in 210 for men and 1 in 124 for women. For men and women in the 40-44.9 BMI (morbidly obese) category at the start of the study, the chance of attaining normal weight in any one year was 1 in 1,290 for men and 1 in 677 for women. That's tiny!

The conclusion was "Obesity treatment frameworks grounded in community-based weight management programs may be ineffective." You're not kidding!

In summary

We know that calorie deficit diets don't work and we've known this for 100 years. We know that people on calorie-controlled diets report horrible side effects, from feeling miserable to feeling cold. We know that something happens at approximately six months – weight loss slows, stops and then reverses. We know that regain often exceeds the initial starting weight, so that people end up heavier than they were before the diet.

We have consistent and repeated evidence for this and yet we meet the definition of madness every Monday morning by starting another calorie-controlled diet and thinking that this time will be different.

I have worked one to one with people to try to help them to lose weight. The first question I ask is – when did your weight problem start? Nine times out of ten, the reply is: "I wasn't that overweight, but I went on a calorie-controlled diet, lost weight, regained it and a bit more. So then I went on another calorie-controlled diet, lost weight, regained it and a bit more." The dieter ended up with a bigger weight problem having tried to diet. In the next chapter, I will explain why.

3
Why 'eat less/do more' doesn't work

"Imagine you're invited to a celebratory dinner. The chef's talent is legendary… Bring your appetite, you're told – come hungry. How would you do it? You might try to eat less over the course of the day – maybe even skip lunch, or breakfast and lunch. You might go to the gym, or go for a longer run or swim than usual, to work up an appetite. Now let's think about this for a moment. The instructions that we're constantly being given to lose weight – eat less and exercise more – are the very same things we'll do if our purpose is to make ourselves hungry, to build up an appetite to eat more."

Gary Taubes[19]

Human beings can be traced throughout evolution to ape ancestors who lived approximately 8-10 million years ago. *Australopithecus* Lucy is believed to be the first upright ape/person – dating back approximately three million years. We are still alive as a species today because we are good at two things: gathering energy and conserving it. If we were only good at one or neither of these, we would have died out long ago. We are here because we are inherently greedy and lazy. We gather food and we conserve it.

Wind forward to the post Second World War modern era and this is the first time in millions of years that we are trying to eat less and/or do more. We are trying to do the opposite of that which we are hard-wired to do. And we wonder why it's not working. Apart from millions of years of evolution, why doesn't 'eat less/do more' work? There are three key reasons:

1. We can't sustain a calorie deficit.
2. Even if we could sustain a calorie deficit, the body adjusts.
3. Trying to eat less/do more makes us eat the wrong things and in the wrong way.

Let's look at each of these in turn...

1. We can't sustain a calorie deficit.

There are a few rare individuals who appear able to sustain a calorie deficit. They are so rare that articles are written about them. Liz Hurley has confessed that the secret to her slim figure is that she goes to bed hungry each night.

I find that sad. I'm every bit as slim as Liz and I never go to bed hungry. There are better ways to stay slim for life.

This is what happens if we try to eat less:
- We get hungry. This is the first thing that happens whenever we start a calorie reduced diet. We try to eat less, but our driver is to eat more – the exact opposite of what we want to happen.
- We have less energy. If we eat less, we have less energy and therefore we want to do less. Our objective was to eat less and do more and yet, as soon as we eat less, our entire driver is to do less – the exact opposite of what we want to happen.

This is what happens if we try to do more:
- We get hungry. The fuel for the activity needs to come from somewhere. Gary Taubes is right. If I want to work up an appetite (before going out for a special dinner), I do some activity. I go for a 20-minute swim or a 30-minute walk and I'm ravenous. We're trying to eat less at the same time as doing more, but doing more makes us hungry. Our driver is then to eat more – the exact opposite of what we want to happen.
- We have less energy. If we try to do more we get tired (especially if we have not matched the doing more with eating more). Our objective was to do more and yet, as soon as we do more, our entire

driver is to do less – the exact opposite of what we want to happen.

Do you see how trying to eat less drives wanting to eat more and do less? Do you see how trying to do more drives wanting to eat more and do less? We can't buck our hardwiring. We can't flip millions of years of evolution just because the diet book says that we should.

There is a fabulous study that illustrates that the body compensates for doing more by doing less at another time. The Department of Endocrinology and Metabolism at the Peninsula Medical School in Plymouth, UK, has been studying a group of 300 children since approximately 2000. The study is known as the "Early Bird Diabetes Study",[20] but it has produced findings for far more than diabetes.

The study picked a random sample of children born in Plymouth between 1995 and 1996. Fifty-four primary schools agreed to take part and 307 children (137 girls, 170 boys, with an average age of 4.9), who started school between January 2000 and January 2001 were selected. The study was designed to try to understand why some children develop diabetes and others don't. However, it has also provided many invaluable insights into obesity and physical activity along the way.

The Peninsula research team have found consistent evidence for the concept of a 'set' activity level. The first study was presented in the *British Medical Journal* (2003).[21]

The participants were 215 children (120 boys and 95 girls, aged 7-10.5) from three schools with different sporting facilities and different opportunities for physical education in the curriculum:

- School 1, a private school with some boarding pupils, had extensive sporting facilities and 9 hours a week of physical education in the curriculum;
- School 2, a village school, offered 2.2 hours of time-tabled physical education a week;
- School 3, an inner-city school with limited sporting provision, offered 1.8 hours of physical education a week.

The research team found that the children with the most scheduled activity at school did the least activity out of school and vice versa. The researchers said of the results: "Surprisingly, total physical activity between schools was similar because children in Schools 2 and 3 did correspondingly more activity out of school than children at School 1."

The conclusion was: "The total amount of physical activity done by primary school children does not depend on how much physical education is timetabled at school because children compensate out of school."

I have observed similar patterns with adults. Those who regularly go to the gym and participate in scheduled exercise classes often have little energy and inclination to be active at other times. They report going to the gym on the way home from work and then "collapsing on the sofa" all evening. Those who don't have the time (or inclination) to go to the gym are more often active throughout the day, on their feet at work, running errands, cleaning, cooking and managing the household.

2. Even if we could sustain a calorie deficit, the body adjusts.

The body can and does adjust to a calorie deficit. Let's see how.

Our energy expenditure is made up of a number of different parts:

- Basal Metabolic Rate
- Physical Activity Level
- Thermic Effect of Feeding
- Non Exercise Activity Thermogenesis

These are all really interesting.

Basal Metabolic Rate (BMR) equates to the number of calories that you need even if you do nothing all day. BMR is by far the biggest part of our daily energy expenditure. It accounts for 45-70% of the energy used by the average person each day. You can estimate your

BMR by using an online calculator. The original Harris Benedict Equation is still as good as any.[22] This uses your gender, age, height and weight to calculate how many calories you need on a daily basis – just to keep your body repair, maintenance and processes going – even if you do nothing else.

For women, the Harris Benedict Equation is:

$$655.096 + 9.563 \text{ W} + 1.850 \text{ H} - 4.676 \text{ A}$$

Where W is weight in kilograms, H is height in centimetres and A is age in years. An average woman aged 40, 5'4" (165cm), 10 stone (63.5kg) thus has a BMR of 1,380 calories a day.

Physical Activity Level is worked out as a factor applied to BMR based on how active you are. Most of us will fall into the sedentary or light activity category, which applies a factor of 1.40-1.69 to the BMR.

If our average woman is at the lower end of this activity scale, she might need 1.40 times her BMR to cover basal needs and her base activity level. This would give her a total energy requirement for the day of approximately 1,933 calories (1,380 x 1.40).

Between 2010 and 2012, I was the nutritionist for a series in the *Daily Mail* called "What I ate yesterday." It was really fun. I was sent the daily food diary for different female celebrities (it was in the Femail section of the newspaper) and I had to say what I thought of their diet. Celebrities included: a number of stars from *Strictly Come Dancing* (Flavia Cacace, Camilla Dallerup, Arlene Phillips, Ola Jordan, Kristina Rihanoff); some Olympic athletes (Sally Gunnell, Paula Radcliffe, Fatima Whitbread, Denise Lewis); stars of *Dancing on Ice* (Katarina Witt, Jayne Torvill); as well as actresses (Joanna Page, Sheila Hancock, Gail Porter); TV presenters (Carol Vorderman, Lorraine Kelly, Gloria Hunniford, Denise Van Outen, Julia Bradbury, Penny Smith, Judy Finnegan) and singers (from Stacey Solomon to Lulu).

What was fascinating to me was how little very active people eat. Paula Radcliffe would start the day with a piece of wholemeal toast and honey and a black coffee and then run 18-20 miles. She would then have brunch – a bowl of cereal, with a banana, more toast and almond butter. Lunch might be an avocado sandwich or sardines on toast. Her regular drink was water – throughout the day. She might graze on a few nuts and then have another run at about 5.30pm (7-9 miles). Dinner was usually something like a home-made fish or chicken curry. My comment was: "This should be a lesson to anyone who thinks that you can eat as much as you want if you are very active. You don't get more active than Paula – still the world marathon record holder and doing a 10-20 mile run before breakfast. Yet how typical is this day's eating – toast and cereal for breakfast, sandwiches for lunch, curry for dinner and a couple of snacks."[23]

Professional dancer, Ola Jordan, had porridge for breakfast, chicken salad or soup for lunch, a couple of lattés, an occasional bag of crisps, maybe some fruit and a pasta supper. That was the fuel for someone highly active for seven hours a day while doing *Strictly Come Dancing*.

This is why I've been saying for years "You can't out-run a bad diet." i.e. what we eat is far more important for weight loss than what we do.

Thermic Effect of Feeding (TEF). When people say that 'a calorie is a calorie', they show that they have no understanding of the thermic effect of feeding. The TEF was first quantified by a Swiss researcher called Dr Luc Tappy.[24]

Food is made up of three things called macronutrients. We know them as carbohydrates, fat and protein. Tappy showed that each macronutrient uses up different amounts of energy to make energy available to the body. He calculated that the TEF for carbohydrate is approximately 5-10%; for fat it is approximately 0-3% and for protein 20-30%. This means that, if we eat, say, 100 calories of pure carbohydrate (i.e. sucrose), then 90-95 of those 100 calories would be available as energy (the other 5-10 would have been used up in making available energy). If we eat 100 calories of fat (e.g. coconut oil or olive oil), then 97-100 of these would be available as energy (only a couple of calories are used up in metabolising fat). The really interesting macronutrient is protein. There is no food that is 100% protein, but egg whites come pretty close. If you consume 100 calories of egg whites (don't – that would be a daft thing to do), only about 70-80 of them would be available to the body.

Tappy proved that a calorie isn't a calorie. We may eat 100 calories, but that doesn't mean that 100 calories are available to the body. More importantly to people trying to lose weight, it also doesn't mean that there are 100 calories to burn off: 100 calories of ice-cream (sugar and fat) do provide almost 100 calories to the body, while 100 calories of fish ends up closer to 80 calories of fuel. I share this not to have you reaching for protein shakes (which would be unhealthy), but to share another reason why counting calories is not a good idea. Calories are different the moment that they enter the body.

Tappy's work is also invaluable as it reminds us about the importance of the quality of food and not just the quantity of food.

Non-Exercise Activity Thermogenesis (NEAT) has been defined as the energy used up doing everything other than sleeping, eating or exercise. It includes the energy expended walking to work, typing, doing house chores, gardening and fidgeting.[25] NEAT seems to have been invented by people who believe calories are all that count, to explain where calories might 'go' if someone seems to eat a lot and not gain weight.

I've seen the concept of NEAT lead to suggestions

that we should constantly fidget to use up more calories throughout the day (which will simply make us hungry!) I remember starting a new job once and having lots of induction meetings arranged with people with whom I would be working regularly. One woman (who I soon discovered was obsessed with eating less and doing more) fidgeted so much during our entire meeting that I thought she had a nervous disorder or a disability. It appeared that she had developed the habit of fidgeting every waking hour to try to use up calories. That's when dieting gets out of hand.

The critical thing to know about all these component parts of energy expenditure is that they can and do adjust when we take in less energy i.e. eat less. As we saw in Chapter 2, the Benedict study published in 1919 showed that a 10% weight loss, from a calorie-reduced diet, resulted in a 37% drop in calories needed thereafter. Men who ate less for a short period of time had a reduced daily calorie requirement thereafter.

Fast-forward 100 years and the DiRECT study referenced in Chapter 1 established that a calorie deficit of one third would need to be maintained to maintain weight loss (let alone to lose more).[26] There's that small print again.

The systems that can (and do) adjust.
I unwittingly did the Minnesota Starvation Experiment aged 15-16. This gave me first-hand experience of what

the body will do to reduce its need for food. With reference to the nine systems of the human body, this is what happened to me within a few weeks of being on a 1,000-calorie-a-day diet (and having lost approximately 20lb):

1. The nervous system, my control room, slowed dramatically and it is astonishing that I managed to study for and take national exams.

2. The skeletal system is likely to have been compromised and I may suffer osteoporosis in later life from the damage caused to my bone density at this time.

3. The endocrine (hormone) system would have gone into minimal operation mode and hormone requirements would have been eased by the shutting down of...

4. ...the reproductive system. At the age of 15 my periods stopped for two years, as my body stopped putting energy into any non-essential bodily operations. It was only after I started to gain weight (involuntarily) and my body detected that I was no longer starving that my menstrual cycle made an irregular return.

5. The digestive system also started a 'work to rule' and I recall very infrequent bowel movements, as there was so little waste to evacuate – my body needed every morsel that it could get.

6. One of the most profound changes that I noticed was with my circulatory system. My extremities were particularly cold and I never felt warm – even at the height of summer.

7. The dual roles of the lymphatic system, drainage of fluids and protection against infection, were obviously compromised as I was puffy, despite being skeletal and I frequently succumbed to colds and flu viruses.

8. I severely tested my urinary system and contracted regular bladder infections, mistakenly thinking that drinking less would make me weigh less.

9. My respiratory system slowed – a friend at a sleepover said that she thought that I had died in the night as I just didn't seem to breathe. My pulse was rarely over 50 despite (or because of?) the fact that I was playing hockey, tennis, rounders and badminton for the school; throwing the discus for the county and swimming to lifeguard standard throughout my teens.

All the bodily systems working together ensured that I fainted regularly. This is the ultimate action that the body can take to try to shock a person into taking corrective action. I cursed these warning signs at the time, in case adults might spot them and force corrective action upon me.

A thousand calories a day is the approximate intake for

millions of people worldwide doing the well-known diet based on points allowances. That we allow this to happen is bad enough. That we are contemplating prescribing slimming clubs as a public health weight loss method, given the impact on the human body, is scandalous.

There is a wonderful anecdote, sometimes attributed to George Bernard Shaw and sometimes to Winston Churchill, which goes along the lines of:

> *Bernard Shaw:* Madam, would you sleep with me for a million pounds?
> *Actress:* My goodness, Well, I suppose… we would have to discuss terms, of course…
> *Bernard Shaw:* Would you sleep with me for a pound?
> *Actress:* Certainly not! What kind of woman do you think I am?!
> *Bernard Shaw:* Madam, we've already established that. Now we are haggling about the price.

I share this because it has much relevance for those who believe that weight is determined by calories in and calories out. Those who believe that we need to create a calorie deficit to lose weight differ only in their view on the level of deficit. The UK National Institute for Care and Health Excellence (NICE) defines very low-calorie diets (VLCD) as those delivering fewer than 1,000 calories a day (some definitions of VLCDs set the bar at 800 calories a day). The NICE definition for low-calorie diets (LCD) is 1,000-1,600 calories a day (other sources define an LCD as 1,200 calories a day or fewer).[27] The UK National Health Service booklet "Your weight your health" advises: "eating 500 to 600 fewer calories each day than your body needs is a realistic way to lose weight. That means around 1,500 calories a day for adult women and 2,000 calories a day for adult men." So, the principle is the same – we're just haggling over the deficit.

A significant calorie deficit is likely to result in short-term weight loss, particularly the first time a person attempts to 'starve'. Weight loss becomes increasingly less successful with further attempts to restrict calorie intake, as the body has no intention of letting the same devastation happen twice. After any initial weight loss, cal-orie intake will need to be continually reduced to try to achieve further weight loss. And the dieter is more likely to have to maintain a debilitating low-calorie intake to avoid the seemingly unavoidable regain. If they manage this, they will be fighting hunger on a daily basis.

The anthropologist Melvin Konner acknowledged this: "There is only one way to lose weight, and that is to grow accustomed to feeling hungry."[28] Konner makes an interesting point here and one relevant to calorie-restricted diets. However, it is completely unacceptable to condemn human beings to a lifetime of being either overweight or hungry. These options are equally intolera-ble and, I believe, unnecessary.

3. Trying to eat less/do more makes us eat the wrong things and in the wrong way.

The third reason why eating less/doing more doesn't work is that even trying to achieve this makes us eat the wrong things.

If we eat less, we try to get the biggest 'bang for our buck' – the most food for the fewest calories. We will therefore choose carbohydrates over fat, because carbohydrates have approximately four calories per gram and fat has approximately nine.

Option A	Option B
1 packet of fruit gums	2 eggs
5 rice cakes	15g butter
2 apples	½ small avocado

As an example, Option A provides one packet of fruit gums, five rice cakes and two apples. Option B provides 2 eggs cooked in 15g of butter with half a small avocado. Both have approximately 400 calories. However, Option B would take fewer than five minutes to cook and could be polished off in a couple more minutes. Option A could be made to last for ages – a fruit gum here, a nibble of rice cake there, a slice of apple when you fancy it.

Because of the calories in carbs compared with fats, and because of how long you can make carb-based foods last, calorie counters become carb lovers and fat avoiders.

The go-to foods for calorie counters are: calorie-counted cereals and cereal products (rice cakes, muesli bars, oat biscuits, crackers, Ryvita etc); endless fruit (just sugar); salads and calorie-counted dressings; fat-free sweets/yoghurts/desserts etc. If any real food is consumed, it is skinless chicken breasts and/or white fish – nothing with the nutrients or satiety of red meat or oily fish.

Option A is 92% carbohydrate, 6% protein and 2% fat. Option B is 7% carbohydrate, 15% protein and 78% fat. Option B is substantially more nutritious and satiating and yet Option A will attract the person trying to eat less.

The pattern of eating for the calorie counter is also seriously harmful. The calorie counter will happily graze all day long – they don't care how many times they eat; they only care how many calories they eat. As we will see in the next chapter, constant grazing is one of the worst things that we can do for our weight and lifelong health.

That's how *trying to eat less makes us eat more carbohydrate*. The same happens if we try to do more – we think that we need to fuel that activity with carbohydrates. You may have heard of the expression 'carb loading'. Marathon runners go out for pizza or pasta feasts the evening before the race, and they have probably been fuelling their training sessions with carbohydrates for the previous months, if not years. There is a growing incidence of very active people developing type 2 diabetes because of this carb loading and because you can't outrun a bad diet.

There's another reason why doing more can be unhelpful for eating patterns. Most of us don't like exercise (we were born to conserve energy, remember) and so we reward ourselves when we have done exercise. A well-known slimming club actively encourages this – you are allowed to reward yourself (the rewards listed are invariably junk) for 'fitpoints', which used to be called 'activity points'. However, you would be better off being functionally fit – doing normal activity as part of your normal daily life (walking to work/the shops, gardening, cleaning, carrying shopping etc) – than doing 20 minutes of something you don't enjoy and then 'rewarding' yourself with junk for the punishment that you just endured. No more doing things that you hate and then giving yourself junk to make it up to yourself!

Just as we opened this chapter, we should close it remembering that we are only here because we've been good at two things: gathering and conserving energy, i.e. eating more and doing less. Yet now, in our obesogenic society, we are trying to buck this hardwiring to eat less and do more. It hasn't worked and it won't work – it's time to do something different...

PART II

What does work?

4

What is weight loss?

"Unless you are a cow, or want to be the
size of one, stop grazing!"

Zoë Harcombe

To understand how to lose weight, we need to understand
what weight loss actually is. That should be obvious, but
astonishingly few people know the mechanism by which
we lose weight. This lack of awareness stems from the
calories in/calories out (CICO) belief. The CICO brigade (I pronounce it psycho!) think that the mere act of
putting fewer calories into the body will magically lead
to weight loss. If only it were that simple. You now know
that the body can and does adjust according to the nutrients it receives.

Body fat is made up of fat cells that are full of tri-
glycerides. Tri means three, as in tricycle or tripod, and
triglyceride is a structure with three fatty acids joined
together with a glycerol backbone. Whenever you see
'glyc' in reference to the body, think sugar, e.g. glycaemic,

glycaemia etc. Body fat is thus three fats joined together with a sugar backbone. To lose weight, we need to break down this triglyceride structure. So, under what circumstances does this happen?

Fuel for the body

The human body has a number of options when it needs fuel. The simplest and easiest fuel to use is glucose. Rare exercise exceptions aside, the body will look for stored glucose when it needs fuel. There are also some organs in the body, for example the heart and liver, which preferentially use fatty acids. But, in general, the body will fuel on glucose if any is available.

Here's a staggering factoid for you: the human body has just 4g of glucose in the entire blood stream at any one time. That's one teaspoon of sugar. If you consume any food that contains glucose (that's any carbohydrate in essence), the body needs to deal with it quite rapidly, because a high blood glucose level can be damaging. Insulin is the hormone, produced in the pancreas, which brings down blood glucose levels. There are a number of ways in which insulin controls blood sugar. It allows glucose to be transported into muscles, where it is stored as glycogen. It also switches on the glucose storage system in the liver, turning glucose into glycogen. In addition to this, it can activate biochemical pathways in the liver

73

that turn glucose into fat.

As I mentioned in the last chapter, marathon runners tend to 'carb load' before a race. They do this to fill up their glycogen stores. The body has the capacity to store only approximately 100g of glycogen in the liver and 250-400g in the muscles. Given that glucose/glycogen is a carbohydrate and that carbohydrates have approximately four calories per gram, that's about 1,400-2,000 calories of glucose fuel that can be stored by the body at any one time. If this glycogen (stored glucose) isn't used within a 24-hour period, the body turns it to fat. Straight away this tells us that the body does not like sugar. It keeps a tiny amount in the blood stream and it doesn't want to store much more in the liver and muscles. Sugar is toxic to the human body. I hope that you're already wondering why we are told to eat so much carbohydrate.

As a general rule, only when the body has run out of glucose will it look for an alternative fuel – fat, for example. The body is quite happy fuelling on fat. However, it finds carbs easier, and our current diet has led to most people having a suboptimal ability to fuel on fat. The body can be retrained relatively quickly and easily. There are a number of writers in the low-carbohydrate world who explain how to help your body to become 'fat-adapted'.[29]

The body has two options for fuelling on fat: dietary fat and stored (body) fat. If you have recently had a butter coffee, for example, your body can use the fat from the butter for fuel. If you are out of stored glucose and out of dietary fat, your body can start to break down body fat. That's weight loss. The body can also break down body fat if your blood glucose level gets low. The body knows that triglyceride comes with fat and a sugar backbone and thus it can break down body fat to get that tiny bit of glucose in the triglyceride structure.

The mechanism by which body fat is broken down involves a hormone called glucagon. Think of insulin and glucagon as equal and opposite hormones. Insulin takes glucose out of the blood stream and stores fuel; glucagon puts glucose back into the blood stream and accesses fuel. These two hormones are antagonists. They are not in play at the same time. If insulin is doing something, glucagon is dormant. If glucagon is doing something, insulin is dormant.

For most people in the so-called developed world, the only time we come close to breaking down body fat, i.e. losing weight, is in the middle of the night when we're asleep. Those people eating the government-recommended 55-60% of their diet in the form of carbohydrate, however, probably never get to this stage. They probably always have stored glucose available as fuel and never need to break down body fat.

For those who eat less carbohydrate, at approximately 4am the body might run out of glucose and start to break down body fat to access the glycerol and to provide some fatty acids for fuel. During the night, you're not eating and so insulin is asleep. Glucagon is thus able to do its job as and when needed.

There are two vital points to make here:

1. If glucose is available, there is no need to break down body fat.
2. If insulin is present, it is not possible to break down body fat.

What makes glucose available? Carbohydrates. What makes insulin present? Carbohydrates again, but also protein. The only macronutrient that doesn't appear to have an impact on glucose or insulin is fat. I hope that you're wondering even more by now why we are told to eat so much carbohydrate.

How to lose weight

There is no guaranteed way to lose weight in that there is no guaranteed way to activate glucagon. However, there are certain things that we can do that make it possible and even probable that glucagon breaks down body fat:

1. Do not have glucose available as fuel.
2. Do not have insulin present.
3. Do things that enable glucagon to be called upon.
4. Don't do things that inhibit the operation of glucagon.

And that's it. That's how to lose weight. Let's take a look at each of these in turn:

1. Do not have glucose available as fuel.
To achieve this condition, you need to consume far less carbohydrate than current dietary guidelines advise. A typical female is currently advised to have 2,000 calories a day and she is advised to consume at least 55% of this in the form of carbohydrate. That would be a minimum of 1,100 calories in carbs per day. The body can only use carbohydrate for fuel. The body can't use carbohydrates for the body maintenance roles, such as building bone density, fighting infection, repairing muscles and cells etc. Those activities require fat and protein. Hence any carbohydrate that you consume needs to be used up as energy, or it will be stored as fat.

You could achieve Condition 1 by trying to eat fewer calories overall and then you might reduce your intake of carbohydrate. But remember what happens here: your body adjusts to the lower intake by doing less; your body makes you hungry; your body drives you to eat more carbohydrate, as you try to get the most food for your measly calorie intake. Keep Chapters 1 to 3 in your head at all times and continually reject the 'eat less' route.

The obvious way to achieve this condition is to eat less carbohydrate and that's one thing that I'm going to be encouraging you to do (although I'll be doing it in a natural way, not in a 'count carbohydrates' way).

2. Do not have insulin present.

To achieve this condition you need to eat far less often than we are advised to do. Current dietary guidelines advise us to eat breakfast, snack, lunch, snack, have dinner and then snack. When are we ever supposed to burn body fat when we are topping up with fuel the whole time? Dieticians advise people to 'eat little and often' and to 'top up your blood glucose'. Now that you know that you only have 4g of glucose in your blood stream at any one time and that more than this is toxic – do you think that this is good advice?

We are told to 'graze'. I give my view on grazing in conference lectures: "Unless you are a cow, or want to be the size of one, stop grazing!"

Every single time that you put something in your mouth that contains carbohydrate or protein (that's everything other than oil or lard basically) you stimulate insulin. Every time you stimulate insulin, you have just made sure that glucagon cannot do anything. You have switched off any chance of burning body fat.

To lose weight, therefore, you need to spend as much of your day as possible not eating and not recently having eaten. I recommend eating a maximum of three times a day if you are trying to lose weight. I say a maximum because some people just don't like breakfast, or find it convenient to skip lunch because of their work, and you shouldn't think that you must eat three times a day if fewer meals work for you.

You may also like to time your meals to give you the maximum overnight fast that you can sustain. I'm an early bird, so I'm often up before 5am in the summer and not much after 6am in the winter. I like breakfast, so I tend to have it quite soon after getting up. I work mostly from home, so I find it easy to have dinner early (and it suits my husband too). Quite often we will have finished dinner by 5pm and usually by 6pm. This means that we have a 12-hour period most days when we are not eating.

There are benefits to this beyond weight loss. Type 2 diabetes is already at epidemic levels and growing. I think that type 2 diabetes is the body's way of saying: "Enough is enough. I cannot cope with the amount of carbohydrate you are eating and the number of times a day you are eating it. I have evolved to cope with seasonal fruit and plants, not to have cereals, muffins, sandwiches, fruit, pasta, pizza and confectionery several times a day, all year round." You will substantially reduce your chance of getting type 2 diabetes if you achieve Condition 1, by eating less carbohydrate, and Condition 2, by eating far less often.

3. Do things that enable glucagon to be called upon.

If you meet Conditions 1 and 2, annoyingly glucagon still doesn't have to swing into action. It is more likely that it will, but it doesn't have to. As equal and opposite hormones, glucagon is the one that we have less control over. Activating insulin is easy – just eat something. Activating glucagon is more difficult. You have to give glucagon a reason to do something.

Once Conditions 1 and 2 are met, the best way to activate glucagon is to increase your need for fuel. Don't think of this as exercise, think of this as functional fitness. You need to do what human beings are designed to do. I described this in my obesity book as "walk, talk, dance, sing, cook, clean and tend the land."[30] If there were a polite verb for sex, I would have included one! This is what we need to do to give glucagon a reason to do its work. And always remember – Conditions 1 and 2 have to be met first or glucagon won't be breaking down body fat.

If you want to fuel a workout, so that your body doesn't have to put in any effort to get energy, eat carbs before the session. If you want to lose weight, don't eat before exercise. One of the best ways in which to enable glucagon is to fast overnight and then start the day with a walk. This is also a wonderful way to wake up and connect with nature. It is probably why dog walkers are slimmer and happier than non-dog walkers. We have no choice about whether to stay in bed when it's cold, dark or rainy. The dog wants a walk first thing and so your raincoat, boots and hat are on before you've even thought – do I want to be doing this?

Don't think of activity as just physical. The brain is one of the most energy-intensive parts of the body. Reading, doing your daily work, doing crosswords or Sudoku puzzles – these activities require fuel and the body will look for some if none is obviously available.

4. Don't do things that inhibit the operation of glucagon.

This is one of the most interesting conditions to discuss because it spears the calorie theory (again) in tandem. Pure alcohol contains approximately seven calories per gram. The calorie theorists think that alcohol will make you fat from the calories it contains. However, the body cannot store alcohol. There is no mechanism by which alcohol per se is turned to body fat. So how can the calories in alcohol make us fat if they can't be turned into fat?

The issue with alcohol is in fact not its calorie content, but the fact that alcohol impairs the operation of glucagon.[31] The body registers alcohol as a poison; and the liver thus prioritises getting rid of the substance before doing the many other jobs that it has to do. This means that maintaining blood glucose levels, by accessing glucose or breaking down body fat, becomes less of a priority.

If you have alcohol in the evening (which is when we tend to consume it), we inhibit glucagon from working for some hours afterwards. Exactly how many hours will depend on how much you've had to drink, how quickly your liver gets rid of alcohol and other individual factors. As a rule of thumb, it takes approximately one hour for the liver to process one unit of alcohol. During the time that the liver is getting rid of the alcohol, you won't be burning fat. Importantly, you won't be burning glucose either because i) the body will preferentially burn alcohol instead of glucose and ii) the liver is too busy dealing with the alcohol to bother with glucose or body fat.

You may have spotted another issue here. Because the body prioritises getting rid of alcohol above regulating blood glucose levels, alcohol drives the munchies. While the liver is processing the alcohol, it is not topping up blood glucose levels and hence they can fall, which makes you hungry. You know this. You know that the kebab van in the alley only ever looks enticing when it's midnight and you've been drinking. In broad daylight, kebabs look distinctly unappetising. This is why some alcoholic drinks are called an aperitif. They are intended to stimulate the appetite before a meal.

When people ask me about alcohol and weight loss, I say don't worry about the calories but do visualise switching off fat burning (weight loss) when you have a drink. You may decide that it's worth it. You may find that a glass of wine, with an early dinner, still gives you some hours overnight when you are fat burning. The choice will be yours – I'm here to give you the knowledge to make an informed decision.

Now that we know what weight loss actually is, let's look at what we need to eat to lose weight.

5
The diet to lose weight

"This magical, marvellous food on our plate, this
sustenance we absorb, has a story to tell. It has a
journey. It leaves a footprint. It leaves a legacy.
To eat with reckless abandon, without conscience,
without knowledge; folks, this ain't normal."

Joel Salatin, Farmer

We're almost ready to set out the ground rules for eating
to lose weight. We just need to explain a bit more about
food…

Macronutrients – fat, protein and carbohydrate

Somewhere along the way we seem to have forgotten why
we eat. We eat because there are nutrients that we must
consume. The word 'essential' in nutrition means 'something that we must consume'. There are essential fats – the
two fatty acids known as omega-3 and omega-6. We need

both of these fats and we need them in a healthy ratio. This is generally recognised as being between 1:1 and 1:4-6 in favour of omega-6, i.e. equal amounts of the two fats, or 4-6 times as much omega-6 as omega-3. Our current ratio is more like 20 times as much omega-6 as omega-3. Entire books have been written about how harmful this could be.[32]

And there are essential proteins – these are the amino acids (component parts of protein) that the body can't make, so they must be consumed. However, it may interest you to know that there are no essential carbohydrates. This is not a controversial statement. It would be accepted by those same public health authorities that advise us to consume most of our calories in the form of carbohydrate – the one macronutrient that we don't need.

Micronutrients – vitamins and minerals

We need 13 vitamins – eight B vitamins, vitamin C and the four fat-soluble vitamins (A, D, E and K) – and we need approximately 15 minerals. The macrominerals (those we need in larger quantities) are: calcium, chloride, magnesium, phosphorus, potassium, sodium and sulphur. The trace minerals (those we need in smaller quantities) are: chromium, copper, iodine, iron, manganese, molybdenum, selenium and zinc.

What food is

I have developed a diagram to explain what food is (in terms of macronutrients) when I speak at conferences:

Carb	Protein						Fat
	Carb/proteins		C/P/F	Fat/proteins			
Sucrose	Fruit/veg	Grains/beans /pulses	Nuts/seeds /avocados	Dairy	Eggs	Meat/ fish	Oils

The above diagram illustrates the following:

1. There is only one 'food' on the planet that is 100% carbohydrate and that is sucrose – i.e. sugar. Arguably it shouldn't be considered a food because it has no essential fats, no complete protein, no vitamins and no minerals. It is simply empty carbohydrate calories.
2. At the other end of the spectrum, there are pure fats. The foods that are entirely fat are oils (olive oil, sunflower oil, coconut oil etc) and lard. Arguably these are not natural foods either. The whole food would be the olive, not a mass of oil extracted from it. Lard is concentrated fat from a pig. The whole food would be a ham joint or pork chop.
3. Protein is in every food other than these extremes

of sucrose and oils/lard. Protein is in lettuce and apples, as well as the more obvious steak and eggs.

4. Nature tends to provide foods that are carbohydrate proteins or fat proteins. Rarely does nature put carbohydrate, fat and protein in the same foods in significant amounts:

i) Carb proteins are foods that come from trees and the ground. These are things that vegans and vegetarians would eat. They include fruit, vegetables, grains, beans and pulses (also known as legumes).

ii) Fat proteins are foods that come from animal sources: meat, fish, eggs and dairy products.

iii) Nuts and seeds are the rare natural foods that contain carbohydrate, fat and protein in significant amounts. This is one of the reasons I advise avoiding these foods if trying to lose weight. The carb fat combo, as I explain in my books about The Harcombe Diet, is uniquely fattening. The carb fat combo is also the domain of processed food – more on this below.

5. As foods are positioned closer to the centre of the diagram, they start to contain more of the macro-nutrient on the other side.

i) Meat and fish are combinations of protein

and fat. They contain no carbohydrate, with the exception of glycogen in liver if you eat offal (which you should). Eggs are also virtually entirely made up of protein and fat – they have just a trace of carbohydrate.

ii) Moving closer to the centre, dairy foods (milk, yoghurt, cheese, cream) are mainly protein and fat, but they can have a measurable carb content. Cream and hard cheese contain very little carbohydrate, but fluid dairy, such as milk and yoghurt, can be as high as 10% carbohydrate. (Please note that dairy products are healthy, but a number of people can be intolerant to them. Interestingly, dairy intolerance is strongly connected to ethnicity. It is not common in northern Europeans, but very common in African Americans and people of Asian origin.)[33]

iii) On the other side of the diagram, fruit and vegetables are almost entirely combinations of protein and carbohydrate. They contain barely any fat.

iv) Moving closer to the centre from the left, grains, beans and pulses do start to contain a bit of fat. Most foods contain at least a trace of fat – this alone tells me that fat can't be bad for us. If the food provided by the planet were trying to kill us, we'd have died out long ago!

How to lose weight

We now have all the principles needed to establish how to lose weight:

Principle 1. Eat real food.

Principle 2. Choose whatever real food you eat for the nutrients it provides (this will naturally manage carbohydrate intake).

Principle 3. Eat a maximum of three times a day.

Principle 4. Manage alcohol intake to enable fat burning.

Principle 5. Do what we're designed to do: walk, talk, dance, sing, cook, clean and tend the land.

Let's take a deeper look at these five principles:

Principle 1. Eat real food. We need to eat food in the form that nature provides it. We have evolved to eat food in that form. We have not evolved to eat processed food with an ingredients list that reads more like a chemistry set. This is the phrase that I use to explain what real food is: "Oranges grow on trees; cartons of orange juice don't. Cows graze in a field; pepperami sticks don't. Fish swim in the sea; fish fingers don't."

You've got the idea.

The list below explains this principle further. Please

note that wheat-based products (flour, cereal, pasta, bread) are not on the recommended 'real food' list, as my experience has been that people lose weight more effectively and feel better without wheat.

REAL FOOD	PROCESSED FOOD
Grains & starch	
Brown rice Oats, quinoa, barley Baked potatoes with the skins on	White rice Bread, pasta, wheat-based cereals, flour Potato chips, crisps
Fruits	
Any whole fruits (eat the skins where edible)	Dried fruits e.g. raisins Fruit juices
Vegetables	
Any fresh, frozen or tinned vegetables with nothing added	Vegetable juices, dried vegetables (vegetable crisps)
Dairy	
Milk, cheese, plain yoghurt (ideally live/with active cultures – the label will tell you)	Milk shakes, ice-cream, flavoured yoghurts, flavoured cheese e.g. cranberries added

REAL FOOD	PROCESSED FOOD
Meat	
Any pure meat (from the butchers or the fresh meat counter in the supermarket) e.g. pork chops, steak, lamb joints, carvery meat etc. Salted/naturally cured meat is also fine – your butcher can guide you to plain cured bacon or ham joints with only salt used as a preserve.	Burgers, sausages (unless made just with meat & herbs/seasoning) Tinned meats often have ingredients added – check the label Sliced packaged meats usually contain sugar/dextrose
Fish	
Any fish from the fishmongers or the fresh fish counter in the supermarket Most tinned fish is OK – tuna, salmon, sardines – any tins with oil, brine and/or water are fine	Processed fish – fish fingers, fish in breadcrumbs (contain white bread and sugar)
Sugar	
Any sugar found naturally in whole food, e.g. fruit sugar in the whole fruit; milk sugar (lactose) in milk	Any sugar, white or brown; maltose, dextrose, sucrose, fructose added to products; treacle; honey etc.
Drinks	
Water, milk, herbal teas	Canned drinks, fruit juice

There is another aspect of choosing real food to consider. Remember that nature tends to provide carb proteins *or* fat proteins? There are a number of reasons why it is ideal to mimic this in the way we combine food. Therefore, I recommend consuming what we call fat meals (fat proteins) or carb meals (carb proteins), but not to mix the two in each sitting. Vegetables, some fruits, herbs, spices and seasoning can be eaten with either type of meal.

FAT MEALS	CARB MEALS
Any unprocessed meat – bacon, beef, chicken, duck, goose, ham, lamb, pheasant, pork, turkey, veal **Any unprocessed fish*** – anchovies, cod, haddock, halibut, mackerel, plaice, pilchards, salmon, seafood, trout, tuna, whiting etc. Includes tinned fish in oil, salt and/or water **Eggs*** **Dairy*** – cheese, milk, butter, cream, yoghurt (ideally natural live)	**All fruit** **Wholegrains** – brown rice, brown rice pasta, quinoa, barley **Whole cereal** – porridge oats, brown rice cereal, other sugar-free, wheat-free cereal, e.g. corn **Beans & pulses** – lentils, broad beans, kidney beans, chickpeas etc. **Baked potatoes in their skins**

* Provided that you are not intolerant to, or allergic to, fish, eggs or dairy.

One of the simple reasons for this is that the carb/fat combination – which is rare in real food yet is the main attribute of junk food – is uniquely irresistible and moreish. Eat cheese with oat biscuits or bread with butter and you may have no limit. Eat cheese with salad, or oat biscuits with hummus, and a far more natural intake follows. Use the tables to adopt the fat/protein or carb/protein meal approach.

EAT WITH EITHER A FAT OR CARB MEAL

Vegetables & salads – alfalfa, artichoke, asparagus, aubergines, bamboo shoots, bean sprouts, beetroot, broccoli, Brussels sprouts, cabbage, carrots, cauliflower, celeriac, celery, chicory, chillies, courgettes, cress, cucumbers, endive, fennel, garlic, green beans, kale, leeks, lettuce, mange tout, marrow, mustard greens, okra, onions, pak choi, parsnips, peas, peppers, pumpkin, radishes, rocket, salsify, shallots, sorrel, spinach, spring onions, squash, Swiss chard, swede, turnips, water chestnuts etc.

Certain fruits – olives, tomatoes & berries

Herbs, spices & seasoning – basil, bay leaves, caraway, cardamom, chives, cinnamon, cloves, coriander, cumin, dill, ginger, mint, nutmeg, oregano, paprika, parsley, pepper, rosemary, saffron, sage, salt, tarragon, thyme etc.

Olive oil or coconut oil for cooking

Principle 2. Choose whatever real food you eat for the nutrients it provides. Now that you know about essential fats and protein, vitamins and minerals, it's time to see which foods provide these.

- Any food that contains fat contains essential fats – only the proportions vary. Oily fish, as an example, is rich in omega-3 fats and has an excellent ratio of omega-3 to omega-6 fats. Sunflower oil is particularly rich in omega-6 fats and thus too much of this can contribute to an imbalance in the essential fatty acid ratio. As a general rule, it is far better to consume fats naturally in whole foods (meat, fish, eggs, dairy etc). For example, the natural form in which to consume olives is the whole fruit; extracting fat from hundreds or thousands of olives is unnatural in my view. It's not as bad as packaged food, but it's still less than ideal. You will spot that the foods naturally rich in essential fats tend to be animal based.
- Protein can be considered complete or incomplete. Complete protein provides all nine essential amino acids that we must consume. Animal foods provide complete protein. Plant foods provide incomplete protein, as they only provide some of the essential amino acids. Plant foods can be combined so that, between them, they provide the necessary amino acids, e.g. rice and beans (as in vegetarian chilli).
- The richest source of micronutrients is offal. If you

want to win a nutrient contest, pick liver. Other foods that do exceptionally well are meat (especially red), fish (especially oily), eggs, dairy products and green vegetables (especially leafy). Sunflower seeds (more of a real food than sunflower oil) are invaluable for vitamin E. If you choose food for the nutrients it provides, you won't choose wholegrains or fruit, which are what dietary guidelines tell us to prioritise.

Sadly for people who would prefer to avoid animal products, the most nutrient-dense foods are meat, fish, eggs and dairy foods. A number of vitamins are only found in foods of animal origin: retinol (which is the form in which the body needs vitamin A); D3 (which is the form in which the body needs vitamin D); K2 (which is the animal form of vitamin K) and vitamin B12.

You can now see how choosing food for the nutrients it provides naturally manages carbohydrate intake. Because you will naturally tend towards fat meals, rather than carb meals. You won't choose porridge, potatoes or rice – there will always be a better food that you can choose (potatoes count as starchy foods, not vegetables).

If you are vegetarian, eggs and dairy products will be your best food choices. If you are vegan, it will be vegetables, beans and pulses. If you put anything starchy on your plate, it is surplus to nutritional requirements. You can have carb meals, but try not to have too many too often and always be aware that you could be eating a fat meal that would be more nutritious.

Choosing food for the nutrients it provides also means that you avoid junk food. Anyone trying to lose weight has no room for empty calories, so ditch the junk and always go for a better option.

Principle 3. Eat a maximum of three times a day. We covered this in Chapter 4 as one of the conditions required to enable your body to break down body fat. Design a meal pattern that works for you and that allows you to spend as much as possible of each day not eating. You may find that your meals need to be bigger and better (more nutritious) than they are now because each one needs to get you through to the next. Principles 1 and 2 will ensure that your meals are optimally nutritious and satiating.

Breakfast should feature: eggs, bacon, smoked salmon or kippers, natural yoghurt and berries – real foods rich in fat and protein and naturally low in carbohydrate.

Lunch and dinner should feature: meat, fish, eggs, cheese, yoghurt, vegetables and berries – again, real foods rich in fat and protein and naturally low in carbohydrate.

Principle 4. Manage alcohol intake to enable fat burning. You may find that you can have a glass of wine on occasions and still lose weight. Or you may discover that it impairs your weight loss so much that it's not worth it. Perhaps keep a food diary and do some trial and error and see what you can get away with. You may decide that you want a night or two a week when you have a glass or two of wine and then you have five or six nights when you've not impaired glucagon.

You'll notice that I have only mentioned wine. Don't go near beer or lager if you're trying to lose weight, as these are more carbs and grains than alcohol and they really won't help. Similarly spirits are mostly grain-based and they tend to come with mixers containing sugars or sweeteners (e.g. whiskey and orange juice). A standard glass of wine, in contrast, has fewer than 4g of carbohydrate. A bottle would start to add up, but you're not going to have a bottle, are you?!

Principle 5. Do what we're designed to do: walk, talk, dance, sing, cook, clean and tend the land. Make the following phrase your way of life: "Eat naturally, move naturally." Take every opportunity to move and do what we are designed to do. The more you do, the more you will be able to do and feel inclined to do. Get into that virtuous cycle as soon as possible.

Don't do any exercise or activity that you don't enjoy – ever. School days are long gone, as are cross country in the rain and navy knickers! If you try to do something you hate i) you won't stick to it and ii) you will think that you deserve a reward and you may be inclined to choose junk. Try new things – you never know what you might find fun. I never thought that I'd like gardening, but I find it really satisfying. I quite like cleaning the house and windows. I can feel my muscles burning, so I know I'm getting some exercise, and then the house looks nicer so I feel virtuous. Paying for a cleaner and a gym membership is madness – the cleaner is getting the best workout!

A weekly plan

Many of you will be happy to adopt these principles and to develop your own menu options to fit with your lifestyle and food preferences. For those of you who like a weekly plan, here's one that integrates Principles 1-4 for you.

The guidelines to accompany the menu plan are:

- You want to get used to eating a maximum of three meals a day. So, eat enough to get through to the next meal without needing a snack. You may find that your portions of meat, fish and eggs need to be more substantial if you are not filling up with (make that fattening up with) potatoes and pasta alongside. It might take a while to get the 'more satiating meals/ no snacks' balance right, so have a real-food snack if need be until you've mastered things. Real food snacks include yoghurt, fruit, boiled eggs, a chunk of

97

cheese, some cold meat from the fridge etc.

- Salads and vegetables (not potatoes) should be enjoyed in abundance. Lunch and dinner should include an array of salads or vegetables – check the list in the tables and be inventive. Our favourite 'super salad' contains: lettuce leaves, cucumber, tomato, celery, peppers, fennel, grated carrot, grated celeriac (in season), with chargrilled onions (for extra crunch) on top. When we have steak, we have mushrooms, spinach, peppers, onions, courgettes and anything else we can find in the veg box.

- Food can be cooked in any of the following ways – roasted, fried (in a dash of olive oil, coconut oil or butter), grilled, baked, poached, steamed.

- Drink as much water as you like (sparkling or still), as well as herbal/fruit teas. Try to cut back on caffeine, if not cut it out altogether, as it has an impact on blood glucose levels. You can have milk in drinks with meals, but not between meals – or you'll be grazing – and never have sugar, of course, or sugary or sweetened drinks.

- Lunches in the menu plan are intended to be easy options that you can take into work in a Tupperware box.

- The menu plan offers simple meal options with minimal prep time. There are full recipes for anything that requires more than assembly on the pages that follow. You will also find hundreds of tasty and nutritious fat and carb meals in our Harcombe Diet recipe books.

- The menu plan only has one course for dinner. You can add fat options to fat meals and carb options to carb meals. For example, cheese (no crackers) or full-fat yoghurt can follow a fat meal. Vegetable soup, or a fruit starter or dessert, could accompany a carb meal. Again – there are many starter and dessert options in our recipe books, or any real-food recipe books that you may have on your shelves.

- Feel free to use the menu plan as a guide, and replace any meal that you don't like with another. Have the same breakfast and main meals every day, if this works for you. There's a good mix of carb (non-shaded) and fat (shaded) meals here. You are likely to find that the fat meals are more filling and that they keep you satiated for longer.

DAY 1:

Breakfast	Bacon & eggs
Lunch	Niçoise salad (see recipe below)
Dinner	Stir-fry vegetables & brown rice (see recipe below)

DAY 2:

Breakfast	Porridge (with water or milk)
Lunch	Brown rice salad (see recipe below)
Dinner	Roast chicken with vegetables or salad (see recipe below)

DAY 3:

Breakfast	Plain Greek (full-fat) yoghurt with berries (strawberries, raspberries, blackberries and/or blueberries. Frozen berries are quite cheap all year round)
Lunch	Roast chicken salad (leftovers from the night before)
Dinner	Vegetarian chilli and brown rice (see recipe below)

DAY 4:

Breakfast	Brown rice cereal (Available in the gluten-free section in super-markets and/or in health food shops)
Lunch	Baked potato & leftover vegetarian chilli (Precook a baked potato when you have the oven on for the roast chicken. Reheat lunch in the microwave at work.)
Dinner	Salmon steaks (see recipe below) or any fish & vegetables or salad

DAY 5:

Breakfast	Plain or ham omelette (see recipe below)
Lunch	Chef's salad (see recipe below)
Dinner	Rice pasta in 15-minute tomato sauce (see recipe below)

DAY 6:

Breakfast	Harcombe protein shake (see recipe below)
Lunch	Fruit platter, plain oat biscuits, cottage cheese
Dinner	Steak or mixed grill with vegetables or salad

DAY 7:

Breakfast	Frittata (see recipe below) or scrambled eggs
Lunch	Roast lamb, pork, beef or chicken with a selection of vegetables
Dinner	Stuffed peppers/tomatoes (see recipe below)

TWELVE EASY RECIPES

Niçoise salad (Day 1)

The original recipe has diced potatoes on top, but omit them here to keep the carbs out of this fat meal.

Serves 4

- 150g green beans
- 4 eggs
- 1 iceberg lettuce, chopped
- 24 cherry tomatoes, halved
- 1 cucumber, diced
- 4 tuna steaks or 400g tinned tuna (or salmon steaks or 400g tinned salmon)
- Olive oil or another dressing
- Salt & ground black pepper

1) Chop the green beans into 3-4cm pieces. Boil them until they are al dente – or to your taste.
2) Hard-boil the eggs (5-10 minutes, depending on how hard you like the yolks). Peel and quarter them when they're cool.
3) If using fresh tuna or salmon, cook it on the barbecue, or in a frying pan or under the grill.
4) Arrange the lettuce, tomatoes and cucumber on 4 plates; add the cooked green beans and hard-boiled eggs.
5) Add a dressing to taste – olive oil is perfect.
6) Place the fish on top.

TIP – add anchovies for extra flavour.

Stir-fry vegetables & brown rice (Day 1)

Allow 50-75g (dry weight) of brown rice per person and 100-150g (precooked weight) of vegetables. Add tofu to make the dish more filling, if you wish.

Long-grain brown rice
Any vegetables you like,
   e.g. onion, garlic,
   baby sweetcorn, mange
   tout, bean sprouts,
   peppers, courgettes,
   carrots, green beans

1) Cook the rice according to the packet instuctions.
2) Clean and chop your chosen mixture of vegetables into bite-sized pieces.
3) Put the onion and peppers into a hot wok, or large frying pan, and stir-fry them until they brown on the edges (you can use a tablespoon or two of olive oil, but none is necessary).
4) Throw in the garlic and then stir-fry for a further 30-60 seconds.
5) Add the rest of the vegetables and toss everything for 2-3 minutes.
6) Then add a soup ladleful of tap water and cook until the water has evaporated. This seals in all the flavour and the good-ness of the vegetables.
7) Stir the brown rice into the vegetables. Season to taste.

TIP: To 'pep' the dish up, add a dash of Tabasco or a pinch of dried crushed chillies.

Brown rice salad (Day 2)

You can precook the rice to make this a quick and easy lunchtime dish. (Make sure that the rice is fully cooked and that you chill it in the fridge immediately after cooking.)

Serves 1

50-75g brown rice
A handful of finely
  chopped salad ingredients
  (cucumber, spring onions,
  peppers, celery, tomatoes,
  spring onions – whatever
  you have to hand)

1 tablespoon olive oil
Freshly ground black pepper
Juice of ½ lemon (optional)
Fresh coriander or basil,
  chopped (optional)

1) Cook the brown rice according to the packet instructions, then rinse it with cold water. Drain it and transfer it to a bowl.
2) In a small cup, make the dressing by mixing together the oil, pepper and lemon juice.
3) Mix the chopped salad in with the rice and then whisk in the dressing. Garnish it with a little fresh coriander or basil if you have some.

Roast chicken with garlic & lemon (Day 2)

You can cook chicken in the oven, in its own juices, with absolutely nothing else but, for more flavour, stuff it with garlic and fresh lemon as follows.

Serves 4
1 medium-sized chicken
6-8 garlic cloves
1 lemon, quartered

1) Preheat the oven to 350°F/175°C/gas mark 4.
2) If the chicken contains giblets, remove them and then stuff the garlic cloves and lemon quarters into the cavity.
3) Cook the chicken breast down for the first 30 minutes to allow the juices to penetrate the breast meat, and then turn it over.
4) Cook it for a further 30-60 minutes. Serve it with a selection of vegetables in the winter or a mixed salad in the summer.

Vegetarian chilli (Day 3)

Vegetarian chilli is a classic recipe that every household cook should be able to dish up. This is a really filling meal and great for reheating when you are in a hurry. As the beans provide decent amounts of protein, it can be eaten as a meal in itself, so don't worry if you don't have time to do rice or a baked potato.

Serves 4-6

2 tablespoons olive oil
2 onions, finely chopped
1 red pepper, deseeded
  & chopped
1 garlic clove, crushed
1.5kg mixed vegetables
  (carrots, courgettes,
  cauliflower, broccoli, leeks),
  cut into 2cm cubes

400g tin of unsweetened
  kidney beans, drained
400g tin chopped tomatoes
2 chillies, deseeded & sliced
Chilli powder to taste
  (2-4 teaspoons)

1) In a large saucepan or wok, heat the oil and gently fry the onions until soft.
2) Add the pepper and garlic and fry for a further 3-4 minutes.
3) Then add all the mixed vegetables, including the kidney beans, tinned tomatoes and chillies and give it all a good stir.
4) Stir in the chilli powder and then put the lid on the pan. Bring it to the boil and then reduce it to a simmer and cook for 20-30 minutes, or until the vegetables are tender.
5) Serve with brown rice, or a crispy baked potato.

Salmon steaks with lime & coriander (Day 4)

The easiest meals comprise quality meat, fish and/or eggs and vegetables. Often a few herbs on chicken or some fennel seeds on a pork chop can really enhance the flavour. This recipe is a prime example of getting a well-sourced salmon steak (ideally from your local fishmonger) and adding just a couple of simple ingredients to transform the basic fish into something with a zing.

Serves 2
2 salmon steaks
Handful of fresh coriander, chopped
Juice and grated zest of ½ lime

1) Place the salmon steaks skin side down in an ovenproof dish and sprinkle the fresh coriander and lime juice over them.
2) Turn them over and pop them under a hot grill for 5 minutes, or until the skin is browned and crispy. Turn the steaks over again and grill them for a further 5 minutes, until they are nicely browned on the other side.
3) Transfer the steaks to warmed plates. Give the juices in the dish a quick stir and spoon them over.
4) Serve the steaks hot with fresh greens or a salad or chill them and enjoy them cold.

Omelette (Day 5)

Omelettes are another dish that should be in the cook's basic repertoire. However, becoming a real omelette master takes patience, creativity and practice.

Serves 1
2-3 eggs
½ teaspoon mixed herbs
Ground black pepper
Knob of butter

1) Crack 2 or 3 eggs per person into a bowl and beat them with a fork, or an electric whisk, until fluffy.
2) Add the mixed herbs and black pepper.
3) Melt the butter in a frying pan and add the whisked eggs.
4) Cook them slowly until they start to set. (You can tilt the pan to move the mixture around to make sure it covers the pan but don't stir it or you will end up with scrambled eggs.)
5) Loosen the edges and fold the omelette over. When it is golden, slide it onto a plate.
6) Serve it with a mixed salad for a main meal.

TIP: for a more substantial meal, add some of your favourite ingredients to the whisked eggs before pouring them into the frying pan. Popular options are ham, cheese and mushrooms.

Chef's salad (Day 5)

This is a base recipe – be your own chef and add in whatever you want – grated celeriac, diced beetroot, green beans – the more colour and nutrients the better.

Serves 4

4 eggs (optional)

Ham, chicken or other cold meats, diced

Hard cheese (such as Cheddar or Edam), diced

1 iceberg lettuce, finely sliced

24 cherry tomatoes, halved

1 cucumber, sliced

4 celery sticks, sliced

4 spring onions, sliced

Red & green peppers, deseeded, cut into strips

1 carrot, grated

Olive oil or another dressing

Salt & ground black pepper

1) Hard-boil the eggs (place them in a saucepan of boiling water for 5-10 minutes, depending on how hard you like the yolks).

2) Cover 4 plates with the sliced lettuce. Arrange the cherry tomatoes around the edges.

3) Scatter the cucumber, celery and spring onions over the lettuce, followed by the pepper strips and grated carrot.

4) Cut the hard-boiled eggs into quarters and arrange them on each plate. Add the meat and cheese cubes.

6) Add a dressing to taste – olive oil with some salt and pepper is perfect.

Niçoise salad

Page 103

Stir-fry vegetables & brown rice
Page 104

Roast chicken with garlic & lemon
Page 106

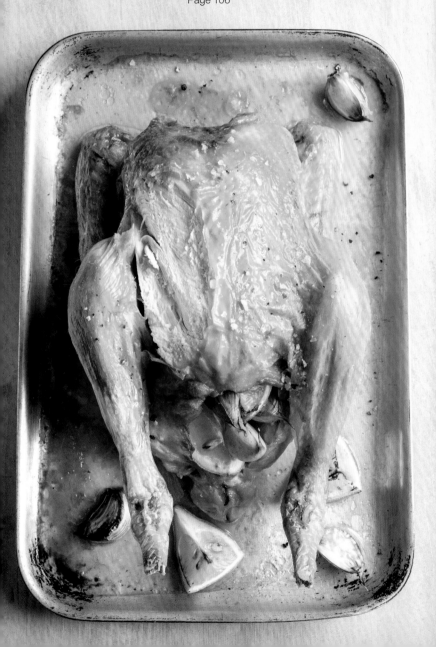

Vegetarian chilli

Page 107

Salmon steaks with lime & coriander
Page 108

Rice pasta in 15-minute tomato sauce

Page 111

Harcombe protein shake
Page 112

Frittata
Page 113

Rice pasta in 15-minute tomato sauce (Day 5)

This is such a versatile sauce. It goes with spaghetti, quinoa, pork chops, fish, chicken, vegetables and tofu, or just about anything else you can think of. Rice pasta is available from the gluten-free section of the supermarket or a health food shop.

Serves 2
100-150g rice pasta
2 tablespoons olive oil
1 onion, finely chopped
1 garlic clove, crushed
400g tin chopped tomatoes
2 teaspoons of basil, chopped
  (or 1 teaspoon dried)
Salt & ground black pepper

1) Cook the rice pasta according to the packet instructions.
2) Heat the olive oil in a wok, or large frying pan, until it is sizzling.
3) Fry the onion and garlic until they are soft (5 minutes) and then add the chopped tomatoes and let them warm through. This will take around 2 minutes.
3) Add the basil, salt and pepper and it's ready to serve.

TIP – to add a spicy kick, stir in a finely chopped chilli with the onion.

Harcombe protein shake (Day 6)

Protein shakes have become increasingly popular of late. The ingredients in shop-bought versions are numerous and many of them are unrecognisable – and therefore they don't meet our real-food principle. Here is a recipe for a natural protein shake – suitable for vegetarians, which you can swap in for breakfast any day.

Serves 2
4 eggs
500ml thick natural live yoghurt
2 rounded teaspoons decaf espresso
  coffee powder

The speedy method is to blitz the ingredients together in a blender and breakfast will be ready in 1-2 minutes. To make the shake lighter and more voluminous, follow these steps:

1) Separate the egg yolks and whites. Put the yolks in one mixing bowl and the whites in another.
2) Using an electric whisk, beat the egg yolks for 1-2 minutes, until they turn pale yellow.
3) Whisk the egg whites until stiff peaks form.
4) Fold the egg whites into the egg yolks.
5) Gently fold the yoghurt into the mixture.
6) Stir in the coffee powder.
7) Serve the shake in a glass, and sprinkle a dash of coffee powder on top.

Frittata (Day 7)

Frittatas are perfect for substantial breakfasts or lunches. This eight-egg version will easily feed two or more. It's lovely cold, so you can save the leftovers for another day.

Serves 2-4

2 courgettes, diced
100g (approx) broccoli,
  cut into small florets
25g butter
4 bacon rashers, diced
  (4 strips of red pepper for
  the vegetarian version)

1 small red onion, finely
  chopped
1 garlic clove, finely
  chopped
8 eggs
Freshly ground black
  pepper

1) Parboil the courgettes and broccoli for 2 minutes, then drain them and leave them to cool.
2) Melt the butter in a heavy frying pan and lightly fry the bacon for 5-7 minutes (or the pepper strips for 3-4).
3) Add the onion and garlic and cook for a further 3-4 minutes, then add the courgettes and broccoli. Cook for a further 3-4 minutes, stirring frequently.
4) Whisk the eggs in a mixing bowl, add some seasoning, pour them over the mixture in the frying pan and pat it all down to form a frittata. Cook it on a low heat for 6-8 minutes, or until it becomes firm.
5) Remove it from the heat and place it under a hot grill until the top of the frittata starts to brown. Then flip the frittata over on a plate for serving.
6) Slice it like a pizza and serve it warm with a mixed salad or your favourite vegetables.

Stuffed peppers/tomatoes (Day 7)

This dish can be made with either peppers or large tomatoes. Use a variety of red, green and yellow peppers to create a lovely colourful dish.

Serves 4
100g brown rice
1 litre vegetable stock
4 peppers (red, green or yellow)
1 tablespoon olive oil
1 onion, finely chopped

1 garlic clove, crushed
4 mushrooms, finely chopped
1 teaspoon mixed herbs
Freshly ground black pepper

1) Preheat the oven to 350°F/175°C/gas mark 4.
2) Cook the brown rice in the vegetable stock for approximately 30 minutes.
3) Meanwhile, prepare the peppers by slicing the tops off and scooping out the seeds from the middle. The idea is to make a 'bowl' with a 'lid' to stuff the other ingredients into.
4) About 5 minutes before the rice is ready, gently fry the onion, garlic and mushrooms in the olive oil until they are soft.
5) Add the herbs and stir in the cooked brown rice. Add some freshly ground black pepper and stuff the mixture into the prepared peppers.
6) Replace the tops on the peppers and place them in an ovenproof dish. Bake them for approximately 20-30 minutes.
7) Serve them with a salad, or on their own.

In summary

To lose weight, we must create the conditions in which we can break down body fat. We now know what these are. We need to give the body every possible reason to burn our love handles for fuel and that isn't going to happen if we're grazing on rice cakes all day long.

- To lose weight, we must eat better – not less.
- To lose weight, we must nourish – not deprive.
- To lose weight, we must change our lifestyle – not go on a diet. Let's turn to how eating better can become our new way of life.

PART III

How to make this your last ever diet

6

The two drivers for change

"Change happens when the pain of staying the
same is greater than the pain of change."

Tony Robbins

There are only two things that make us change. We move
away from pain and we move towards pleasure and that's
it. We are hungry (pain), so we hunt for food. We find
some ripe berries (pleasure), so we eat them. These two
fundamental drivers control all animal behaviour. My cat
moves away from foxes and other tom cats, as he doesn't
want the pain of getting hurt. He moves towards me for
food and fuss and to the radiator for warmth and that's
his pleasure sorted. Human beings are the same – we just
have a more intelligent understanding of pain and pleasure and more control over our environment to be able to
achieve both.

Over the years of working first as a human resources
director and now as a nutrition writer and speaker, I
have come to realise that the fear of pain is a far greater

motivator than the desire for pleasure. Meeting several hundreds of people, who have changed their lifestyle, has confirmed that to be the case.

A significant proportion of people who have signed up to real-food/managed-carbohydrate diets have done so after having been diagnosed with type 2 diabetes. Others have been motivated to change by a heart attack; their own or one in the family. Being too overweight to play with one's children is a powerful pain driver. There are many people in our online Harcombe Diet club who started healthy eating to lose weight and look better (pleasure), but they sustained the change because they feel so good, i.e. they don't want to revert to the pain of ill health, which they now recognise they were previously suffering. If you think about the people you know, who have made significant dietary changes, has pain or pleasure been their greater motivator in your experience?

Have you watched any of the BBC television *Doctor in the House* programmes? The idea was that a general practitioner, Dr Rangan Chatterjee, would move into different households to observe first-hand the health behaviours of the family members. Some of them seemed healthy; others clearly had distressing conditions such as obesity, immobility or pain. For months, if not years, before the programme was even conceived, the families had many pleasure reasons to change their behaviour. Long before Rangan arrived, they could have been inspired to adopt a healthier lifestyle to look younger or slimmer. They could have been motivated by the prospect of feeling fitter, or having more energy, but they weren't. The diagnosis of type 2 diabetes, or the fear of cancer, was the pain that ultimately drove change.

New Year resolutions

A 2017 survey of American adults found that 41% of people usually make New Year's resolutions, 42% never do and 17% make them infrequently.[34] Just 9% of people felt that they were successful in achieving their resolution. The most common resolution was to lose weight/ adopt healthier eating. One in five people (21%) had this as their New Year resolution. This was almost double the second-most common resolution – to make general life/ self improvements (12%).

The rest of the top 10 resolutions were: three – better financial decisions; four – quit smoking; five – do more exciting things; six – spend more time with family/ friends; seven – work out more often; eight – learn something new on my own; nine – do more good deeds for others; ten – find the love of my life.

	RESOLUTION	% OF PEOPLE
1	Lose weight/healthier eating	21.4%
2	General life/self improvements	12.3%
3	Better financial decisions	8.5%
4	Quit smoking	7.1%
5	Do more exciting things	6.3%
6	More time with family/friends	6.2%
7	Work out more often	5.5%
8	Learn something new on my own	5.3%
9	Do more good deeds for others	5.2%
10	Find the love of my life.	4.3%

For most people, the number one resolution – to lose weight – would be a pleasure, rather than a pain, motivator. In fact, all of these top 10 resolutions are substantially gain, not pain, goals. 'Quit smoking' may be a pain (health fear) goal, but it is still likely to be a gain goal (save money, clothes smell better, anti-social habit etc) in the all important short term. Maybe that's why so many people fail – they don't have the most powerful driver for change on their side.

If you want to be in the 9% of people who do achieve their resolutions, you need to understand your driver for change.

The thing about the pain driver and New Year resolutions is that pain does not conveniently coincide with a random date in the calendar. The health diagnosis rarely occurs on 31st December – leaving someone with the ultimate reason to change the day after. Pain drivers can occur at any time of the year and those are the powerful ones to respond to the minute they do occur. The tragedy is that prevention is so much easier than cure and yet human behaviour is more inclined to react, than to prevent.

Long-term evidence for public health interventions

Each nation has public health bodies, the role of which is to improve the health of citizens and to save national expenditure on health care by preventing illness. Such bodies and their staff seek to motivate people to make lifestyle changes, so that ill health can be avoided and the accompanying burden on the public purse reduced.

The best evidence for long-term public health interventions must be the 2013 publication from the Caerphilly cohort study.[35] The Caerphilly cohort study started in 1979 with the recruitment of 2,235 men aged 45-59. Their healthy behaviours were recorded and the men were then followed for 30 years to record incidents of, and deaths from, diabetes, heart disease, cancer and other illnesses.

This long-term population study found that there are

five healthy behaviours that are most strongly associated
with good health:

- Not smoking
- Maintaining a BMI in the normal range (18.5-
  24.9kg/m2)
- Consuming three or more portions of fruit and vege-
  tables a day (likely a marker of a generally good diet)
- Taking regular exercise
- Maintaining alcohol intake within sensible limits

Compared to men who followed none of the five healthy
behaviours, men who followed four or five had half the
incidence of diabetes, half the incidence of heart disease
and two thirds of the incidence of cancer. Men who followed four or five healthy behaviours had just 40% of the
deaths from any cause (during the study period) compared to the men who followed none.

The fascinating and most significant finding of this
study, however, was that not even one in 100 men followed all five healthy behaviours; just one in 20 followed
four or more and that this did not change between 1979
and 2009. In 30 years of studying these men, the proportion of them adopting a healthy lifestyle was tiny and did
not improve over time. The lead author, Professor Peter
Elwood, described this as a damning indictment of the
value of public health policy.

What we don't know from this study was – did people

change their behaviour when they experienced pain? Did a diagnosis of type 2 diabetes, or cancer, or a heart attack, or some other health scare elicit change? We don't know. What we do know is that not many people are following healthy lifestyles and public health interventions have not changed this in three decades.

A 2018 paper reviewed data from two US studies – the Nurses' Health Study (1980-2014) and the Health Professionals Follow-up Study (1986-2014) – and reached the same conclusions as the Caerphilly study.[36] The US review looked at 34 years' worth of data. The same five healthy behaviours were found:

- Never smoking
- BMI in the normal range
- A high diet quality score
- A minimum of 30 minutes moderate to vigorous physical activity per day
- Moderate alcohol intake

Adherence to all five healthy behaviours was estimated to extend life expectancy at age 50 by 14 years for women and 12.2 years for men, compared with individuals who adopted none of the lifestyle factors.

Why don't we choose health? When Christopher Reeve became paralysed from the neck down in a horse-riding injury, he said in an interview that he would swap the fame and wealth that he had achieved for the ability to walk again. We take health for granted until it is taken away from us. We have a natural optimism that makes us think we will win the lottery (why else would we buy a ticket?), but that we won't be the one in two or three people to get cancer. It seems that the fear of pain is not enough as a motivator; we need to experience the pain to be motivated to change. We know that diabetes leads to complications such as amputations and blindness. But unless we have diabetes, we don't think about such things. Many people with diabetes still don't think about such things. It took Geoff Whitington, in *Fixing Dad*, the likelihood of amputation to inspire change.[37]

Inspiration from those who have changed

I have had the privilege of helping people to lose weight and gain health since 2004 when my first book was published. As part of the research for this book, I asked a number of the people who have achieved and maintained life-changing weight loss: "What finally motivated you to change?"

There were many pain drivers. One of the most serious and heartfelt came from Christelle. She summed up her motivation to change as "fear".

Fear of premature death, not seeing my daughter grow up and not being able to do certain things with her because I was too big. The fear of having a debilitating disease; of losing limbs or brain function due to that disease. The fear of not being able to walk because I am so heavy my legs can't support my weight. (This is prevalent in my family. A lot of my aunts battle with this issue.) This all fell into place in 2016 when I could not walk for a couple of kilometres without wanting to cry because my back was hurting so much. At that stage my blood pressure was through the roof and I remember thinking I am going to have a stroke if I do nothing about my blood pressure.

Reading *Stop Counting Calories & Start Losing Weight*, the thought that went through my mind was: 'I am going to try this. What do I have to lose?' I was very sceptical to start off with because you hear all these great and wonderful things that will help you lose weight and here someone is telling you what to do and it seems so simple. Just eat real food. Can it really be that simple? I am a testament of this. Yes, it really is that simple. After losing a lot in week 1, I knew I was hooked.

'Sistercas' was motivated by the threat of type 2 diabetes, as her blood glucose levels were getting close to the threshold, and the realisation that she was just out of control with her eating.

Anne was shocked into change by her husband's diagnosis of type 2 diabetes. She knew that this could be substantially helped by diet, rather than drugs, and so took charge of a new family way of eating. Anne herself had gained weight and lost health over the years and so was in the right place at the right time for her husband's health scare to motivate change for both of them.

Christine has a genetic weight condition, not unlike lipedema, and came to realise that some things would be out of her control, but that she could still be the best that she could be. Her commitment to real food and managed carb intake (which for her condition needs to be very low) is awe-inspiring.

Mat vowed to change when he realised that he was getting "too fat to run around with his kids". He thought that he owed it to them to lose weight and gain health.

Jules found that she was struggling to bend down to cut her toenails and then saw some unflattering holiday photos and said "enough is enough". Jules looked so amazing after her lifestyle change that she was featured in a glamorous photo shoot for a glossy fashion magazine.

Jen's life was being blighted by horrific migraines, which cleared up, as did many other ailments, when she ditched her (well-known) slimming club for a real-food lifestyle.

A number of people simply got 'fed up' (that is such an appropriate metaphor) with how they felt: overweight, out of control with food and sick from the junk being consumed.

Carol was fed up with chronic heartburn and having

to take antacids all the time. Eating real food has fixed her weight, heartburn and general health all in one.

Linda simply said: "I got sick and tired, literally, of being addicted. Fed up with being unable to say no, even when I knew I wasn't enjoying it."

John had been fed up with his weight since his teens and had lost weight and regained over the years (with calorie deficit diets). He just wanted something that worked "once and for all". He wanted a lifestyle change – no more diets – and he has never looked back since choosing to eat better, not less.

Tracy wanted support as the menopause loomed and early symptoms of peri-menopause were making her life miserable. Eating better has made her feel better. She also wanted to look great at an event with her husband and the idea of nothing fitting inspired her to change. Tracy's reaction to possibly being a size 20 was "I'm not having that!" She was also inspired by tragedy – the loss of a relative at just 31. This often helps people to establish better and more meaningful goals. Death can help us to see the bigger picture of life.

Although, as we've seen, pain drivers are the best motivators, there are some pleasure drivers, which can also be very powerful, e.g. events such as weddings, graduation ceremonies and school reunions. A wedding inspired Rosemary to change: "I was coming over to a wedding (from Australia to England) and had purchased the expensive outfit months in advance. I knew I needed to lose a few kilos to make it look better. Instead I gained another five. So, seven weeks before the wedding, I had an urgent need to drop the excess. At this time a friend loaned me *The Harcombe Diet: 3-step Plan* and the rest is history. I lost my 8kg and subsequently another 14kg."

'Weebear' described her initial motivation as "vanity" – there's absolutely nothing wrong with that. For her, size 16 was the mental break point. When Weebear realised that this was the size she was trying to squeeze into, and that she generally felt bloated and had a poor complexion, she reached her 'enough is enough' moment. She ditched sugar, alcohol and caffeine. She lost weight, feels great, eats really well and is thrilled to be setting a good example for her children. Her only regret is not starting the real-food way earlier.

Size also motivated Bethan. She had her watershed moment when she bought a size 18 top. She went from thinking of herself as "a bit overweight" to being "a fat person" (her words). She's now been a size 8-10 for years and loves it.

In the next chapter we are going to build on what we've discovered about the drivers for change to make sure that you too can reach your goals.

7

How to make this time different: values, goals and beliefs

"Change will not come if we wait for some other person or some other time. We are the ones we've been waiting for. We are the change that we seek."

Barack Obama

If you are unhappy with your health and weight right now, let me assure you, I've been where you are. I've been overweight, feeling addicted to and out of control around food. I've lurched from one sugar high to sugar low, feeling hyper one minute and exhausted the next. I've started days vowing to do things differently and then found myself eating a muffin at 11am.

I know what you're going through and I'm now going to share with you how to get to where you want to be...

Accept that only you can do this

When I was in a bad place I was always looking to the next person who could help me. I'd see a nutritionist in a magazine and be convinced that this was what I needed. I'd see an advert for a hypnotherapist and be convinced that they could programme me to loathe chocolate (as if!). I spent too long thinking that someone else could help me when the only person who could help me was there all along – me!

People can help. I can help. Books and knowledge can help. The support of friends and family can definitely help. But the only person who can change you is you. The day that you realise this is the day that you can take the first step down the road of being the person that you want to be; the person that you really can be.

From this point on, it will help to have a notebook by your side. I'll be recommending that you make some notes to keep and refer back to, so get a nice notebook – as special as the insights that you are going to make.

Please take a moment to review all the occasions when you have been inspired by something someone has said or done. Get out all your self-help books if need be and make a note of the best tips that might help you on your journey. Write down the names of all the people whose help you have tried to enlist – whether a counsellor, doctor, coach or nutritionist. Capture the best points that each of them have made – the tips that might help you.

Think of people who have inspired you – friends, family members or celebrities who have achieved change and earned your admiration.

Now is the time to gather all the knowledge and inspiration that you have acquired up to this point and see it for what it is – stuff that can help you to help yourself. Own what happens next. Understand and accept that only you can change you. Write down a statement that you will sign and commit to. For example, this is the statement that I wrote to myself over 20 years ago:

I vow that I am going to eat for health and weight. I commit this minute to eating real food – if nature didn't provide it, I'm not going to eat it.

I care passionately about my health and not just my weight. I absolutely do not want weight gain, bloating, depression… I loathe feeling foggy, feeling hopeless and feeling helpless… I will not put up with having my energy, weight and health trashed for even one stupid moment of madness.

My commitment to health and weight starts today – and I mean today – not tomorrow. Tomorrow really does never come. By making this commitment today, tomorrow will be easier and the day after that easier still and I love the idea that I will then be on a positive journey and not a horrible nightmare.

132

I will get slimmer and healthier starting today. That's my commitment to the most important thing in my life – me!

Please use this and/or change it and/or write your own statement. Take your time. This is life-changing stuff. The day that I accepted that only I could change my life is the day that I started to change my life. You can do the same – right here – right now; you just need to firmly own the fact that, as Obama said, you are the one that you've been waiting for.

Understand your why (and what you're prepared to do to achieve it)

Now that you know that there are only two drivers for change – pain and pleasure – which is yours going to be? Knowing that pain is the stronger of the two drivers – do you have a pain motivator that you can harness? Is there a family history of a condition that you can bring more to the forefront of your mind?

If you are more than a little overweight… if you have a particularly large waist size… if you find yourself craving sugary and starchy foods to try to get a brief energy boost before a crash… you may well be at risk of type 2 diabetes. You can get tested by your doctor. You can even buy home testing kits, if you want to just see for yourself. The most reliable test is not a urine sample (which only tells you if you have high sugar in your urine at the moment). A measure called HbA1c gives you an idea of your blood glucose levels over the past three months, making this a far better indicator of your general levels. You can get finger prick home testing kits online, which will be a reasonable guide, but a blood test done by your doctor will be more accurate.

A crisis may be the biggest driver for change, but surely it would be so much safer to change before the crisis happens? If only we hadn't waited until the tragedy of Grenfell Tower before discovering that the cladding on many tower blocks was highly flammable. If only the co-pilot of the flight trying to leave Tenerife-North airport in March 1977 had had the confidence to speak up, while sat next to the 'poster boy for KLM' captain who was impatient to take off. The crisis was foreseen, but the changes that could have prevented the deaths of 583 people that day didn't happen in time.

Can you see the pain that is coming if you continue on your current path? Can you commit to making life-enhancing change now – before you crash? You're probably already in a greater place of pain than you might think. Write down everything troubling you – excess weight, cravings, disturbed sleep, headaches, bloating, energy highs and lows, missing out on social events. Write down everything that is spoiling your quality of life at the moment – that's the pain that you want and need to move away from. Harness it, hold it, don't forget it – until it's gone.

Just because pain is stronger doesn't mean that pleasure can't be a powerful motivator. The revenge diet is a highly successful one! If you get dumped by a partner, there is no limit to the joy of turning up at an event where s/he will be and looking like the 'after' photo in the before and after transformation. If you were 'the overweight child in the class', imagine walking into the school or college reunion looking a million dollars, and then make it happen.

If you weren't always 'the overweight one', get out a photo where you looked great. It will elicit a mixture of pain and pleasure motivation. You will feel pain that you don't look like that now – let that pain motivate you. You can have the pleasure of looking like that again – let that gain motivate you.

Can you mix pain and pleasure as Bethan and Weebear so nicely described in the last chapter? Is there a number on the scales that will give you your 'enough is enough' moment? Is there a clothing size looming that is simply unacceptable to you?

Remember Mat, Tracy and co? A number of the motivators they shared involved other people. Mat wanted to be able to play with his children. Tracy wanted to make her husband feel proud at a special event. Overweight people are often the carers and helpers in this world. It may seem selfish to these people to set a personal goal – a priority no less, to put above everything else and maybe everyone else. Such a person might be more motivated by a 'why' that is for someone else. I want to be my best for my partner/family. I want to be around for my children. I want to look fabulous at my daughter's graduation ceremony.

Whatever you're about to do, you need to understand your why. What do you want to achieve? Why do you want to achieve it? This exercise may make you realise that actually you're happier with where you are than you realised – in which case, embrace this newfound contentment and enjoy being essentially where you want to be.

You are going to have to make some sacrifices on this journey to better weight and health. There will be times when you want to have your cake and to be slim. You will be able to have some 'cheats' (we call them cheats, not treats – we need to break with the view that junk is good for you), but you will come to realise that the fewer you have, the fewer you will want and the better you will look and feel. You will need to be strong at the point of choice, so you may as well be honest now. If getting drunk and having takeaways a few times a week is more important to you than looking and feeling great, be honest now and save yourself the bother. There will be temptations all the time (the longer you resist temptation, the easier it is to resist), so you need to know that your long-term 'why' will beat that short-term 'urge'.

Dr Jen Unwin is a wonderful psychologist, whom I

have got to know through speaking together at food and health conferences. Jen asks her patients two questions: i) "What would you like to achieve?" and ii) "What are you prepared to do to achieve it?" This is a brilliant way to enable both Jen and the patient to predict an outcome. The answers to these questions will reveal if the patient's goal is realistic and if they are prepared to put the effort in to achieve it. If the patient wants to manage type 2 diabetes without medications, but isn't prepared to change their diet, Jen can be honest and tell them this won't work. Either the goal, or the commitment to it, needs to change.

If your heart sinks because you think that you aren't prepared to put in the effort necessary to achieve your goal, don't lose hope just yet. Chapter 9 may be enlightening to you. In it, I will share insights into the importance of our psychological make-up. We have all had different backgrounds and upbringings. You may have been brought up in a 'permissive' way and you may have had everything handed to you on a plate (another great metaphor). Just knowing this may inspire you to change your view of what you are prepared to do to achieve your goals.

What do you want to achieve and what are you prepared to do to achieve it? Have you got your 'why'? Have you captured your pain and/or gain? Great – because we're now going to make your 'why' SMART...

Set SMART goals

My corporate background and weight-coach role coincide here. In business, there is an acronym for setting goals called SMART. Goals need to be Specific, Measurable, Achievable, Realistic and Timebound.

Specific means that your goal needs to be as clearly described as possible. You should be able to share your goal with a stranger, such that they know exactly what you're aiming to achieve. For example, I want to be able to wear my favourite jeans again. I want my blood glucose levels in the normal range. I want to be able to wear a swimsuit on holiday.

Measurable means that you will be able to monitor progress. For the blood glucose goal example, you may start with an HbA1c of 53mmol/mol (7%) and set a goal of below 42 (6%). You will be able to measure progress along the way. If your goal is to lose x pounds/kilos, you will also be able to measure this along the way.

Achievable means something that you can achieve. The great thing about personal health goals is that they are almost always achievable. In business, your goal may not be achievable because of other people or the organisation itself. For example, most Accident and Emergency doctors would love no one to wait more than a few minutes to receive emergency care. This is sadly not achievable because demand for help is so much higher than the supply of that help (doctors, beds and funds). Provided that your goal is realistic, you will be able to achieve it.

Realistic means what it says. A fitness goal doesn't have to be 'run a marathon'. Get a pedometer; see how many steps you are currently doing and try to do more tomorrow and the next day and so on until you reach a few thousand a day. The diet goal doesn't have to be 'organic everything and below 25g of carbohydrate a day'. Start with 'eat real-food' (meat, fish, dairy, eggs, vegetables, fruit in season, brown rice, oats etc) and master this first. Then you can reduce carb intake to see what is optimal for your weight, activity and health.

If a particular weight is your specific goal, check what this means in terms of BMI. If your goal weight means that you would end up with a BMI of 19, it's not realistic. If you're a tall male and you've never been below 200lb/90kg in your adult life, you're probably not going to get there now. You can always carry on once you've achieved your goal, but set a realistic one from the beginning.

Timebound means put a timescale on it. This is particularly important with weight and health goals because those are the ones we always want to start tomorrow. If you want to knock them dead at the college reunion, get your specific goal and then work out what measurements you need to achieve along the way to make it happen.

My brother is a massive cricket fan and I always think of goals in 'run rates'. In limited-over cricket, the second team to bat knows how many runs it needs to get in how many overs. This establishes a run rate. For example you might need to get 200 runs in 50 overs, which means you need to keep up an average of four runs an over. Anything below this and the pressure will get bad towards the end of the match. If you can hit a few great shots early on in the chase, your run rate may drop to two or three, which really takes the pressure off. Think of timebound targets in the same way – don't leave it until the last week before the reunion to try to lose 20lb. Get a cracking start, keep chipping away over the following weeks and then you can start planning your outfit with confidence.

Your SMART goals need to be written down and clearly captured – ideally in the same notebook where you have captured you personal commitment statement.

Before we leave the goals section, I just want to check that you're focused on one SMART goal. If your to-do list has become: quit smoking; learn a new language; go to the gym; and eat no sugar or white flour... these are all admirable goals, but you will not achieve them all. You'll probably achieve none of them, because your resolve will be spread too thin. Pick one thing and put all your effort into it. When this one thing becomes a habit (second nature), then – and only then – pick another thing. You can be the smoke-free, Paleo, six-pack Spanish speaker, but only if you master and embed goals one at a time.

Understand your beliefs – especially your limiting beliefs

My friend Hayley is a high-level business coach. She gets called in by global corporations, usually when they're at crisis point, to help the organisation and the people within it to change. She is brilliant at what she does. She told me a funny and memorable way of understanding beliefs...

Have you ever watched *X-Factor*, *American Idol* or *Britain's Got Talent* in the early stages of the competition? Can you remember the most cringeworthy auditions when someone appears before the judges and they clearly think that they are a great singer or super dancer and they're not? They start to sing or move and we don't know whether to laugh or cry because they are so bad! Here's the thing – the person doesn't think that they're bad. Quite the opposite – they genuinely look astonished when the judges say that they were rubbish. Their beliefs are wonderful and uncommon. They are among the rare human beings who think that they have a talent that they don't. That's the power of beliefs, Hayley explains.

Too many of us – women especially – have talked ourselves down over so many years that we have lost all connection with our strengths and even our souls. We probably didn't start this. We may have had overly critical parents or teachers or a sports coach for whom nothing was ever good enough. We may have started the bad scripts in our own heads by comparing ourselves with others at school or at activity clubs. Why is it that we rarely compare ourselves with those below average and feel good? We are more likely to compare ourselves with the best and feel bad.

The voice we hear most often throughout our lives is our own. The person who delivers the most messages to us – good or bad – is our self. We will have picked up many beliefs since our first consciousness and we will have reinforced these over time. The great news is – just like a DJ – we can change the record any time we like. It's not easy, but it's also not as difficult as you might think.

The first thing that you need to do is write down (back to that notebook) as many beliefs that you have about yourself that you can think of. Don't judge yourself as you write them down. Don't think about whether they are good or bad – just capture them. There are some examples in the box opposite. You will see that they are a mixture of attributes (kindness, perseverance etc) and skills/competencies (numeracy, languages, cooking etc).

POSITIVE BELIEFS	LIMITING BELIEFS
I am kind	I am cruel
I am a good friend	I let friends down
I am hard-working	I am lazy
I persevere	I give up
I concentrate well	I am easily distracted
I am good at maths	I am bad at maths
I am good at languages	I am bad at languages
I am generally happy	I am generally unhappy
I can cook	I can't cook
I am pretty healthy	I am always sick
I feel in control	I feel out of control
I can say no	I can't say no

Put a big tick next to all the positive beliefs that are relevant to you. Put a tiny cross next to all your limiting beliefs. If you have far more limiting than positive beliefs, text your best friends and ask them to tell you the personal qualities and skills that you have that they admire and then add them to your list whether you agree with them or not (who are you to think you know better than your friends?!)

Next you need to look back at your SMART goal and circle any and every belief that can help you towards your goal and underline any and every belief that is going to get in the way of you achieving your goal.

As this book is about getting you slim and keeping

you there, the beliefs that will help will be things like: perseverance, feeling in control, being able to say no etc. The beliefs that won't help will be things like 'I give up', 'I am lazy', 'I can't say no'. We need to harness the power of our positive beliefs. More importantly, we need to change our limiting beliefs. We will never get to the self-delusion of the *X-Factor* wannabe, but we must get to the place where our beliefs accurately reflect the best of who we are.

The best model I have come across, to change a belief, habit or behaviour, is:

The four stages of competence model

Also known as 'conscious competence' learning model, this was first presented by Martin M. Broadwell in an article about Christianity called "Four stages of teaching" in 1969.[38] The model is an effective and memorable way of understanding the four stages that we need to go through to change behaviour. The stages are:

1. Unconscious incompetence

At this stage, we are doing something wrong, but we don't even know that we are. Our incompetence is not conscious. This is the stage of bad habits – where we can engage in unhelpful behaviour and not even realise it. We think we're sticking to our diet; we don't register the crisps or chocolate that we can consume when we're engrossed in a screen (TV, phone or computer).

2. Conscious incompetence

This is the first stage along the process of change. We need to force ourselves to become aware (conscious) that we are doing something wrong (incompetence). At this stage, we still exhibit the bad behaviour, but we have become aware of it. We catch ourselves grabbing a bag of crisps before sitting down to watch TV. We realise that a bar of chocolate has gone while we've been watching cat videos on YouTube. We need to catch ourselves doing it every time, so that we can start to change this behaviour.

3. Conscious competence

After a while, we become consciously competent. We still have to think very carefully and work hard to do the right thing, but we increasingly do the right thing. We make sure that no food or drink is within reach of the computer. We arrive at the cinema just in time so that we don't get a bucket of popcorn.

4. Unconscious competence

The final stage is when we do the right thing, naturally, without even thinking about it. We have reached the level of habit – that's when 'no mindless eating' is second nature. It would no longer occur to us to ever eat or drink in front of any screen. This resolution is now nailed and we can move on to the next.

In summary

The four stages of competence model is your tool to use freely to change your life. You can't change a bad habit unless you know that you have a bad habit. You can't improve something unless you know that something needs to be improved.

This chapter is about owning the change that you want to achieve. It's about understanding why you want to change and what you're prepared to do to achieve it. It's about setting SMART, not vague, goals – something that you can genuinely strive for and know when you've achieved it. It's about honestly examining your beliefs – those that can help you and those that are harming your progress – and then using the four stages of competence model to change anything getting in the way of your end in mind: one bit of 'incompetence' at a time.

8

How to make this time different: learning from past mistakes

"If you live long enough, you'll make mistakes. But if you learn from them, you'll be a better person. It's how you handle adversity, not how it affects you. The main thing is never quit, never quit, never quit."

Bill Clinton

"All men make mistakes, but only wise men learn from their mistakes."

Winston Churchill

The last chapter was about how to get your goals, values and beliefs in place. This chapter is about overcoming obstacles that may derail you.

Your notebook will have your personal statement and your key driver – whether a pain or pleasure. Your

SMART goals will be written down, as will your beliefs. The positive ones are being harnessed and any negative ones are being subjected to the four stages of competence, so that you move to unconscious competence as soon as possible.

We now need to address some other things that could get in the way of you achieving your SMART goal. Let's start with experience – what has happened before.

Experience

Like Oprah, you will have been on many diets. You will have succeeded at some, if not many. However, you're reading this book, so you are still not where you want to be. Mistakes are only mistakes if we fail to learn from them.

Use your notebook to make a note of the reasons why you have 'failed' in the past. Every experience of something going wrong is a gift – an opportunity to learn, so that you can avoid making the same mistake again. In my experience of working with people to succeed at weight loss, past mistakes fall into five main categories:

1. Doing the wrong diet.
2. Not getting expected results.
3. Food addiction.
4. 'Weakness' at the point of choice.

5. Environmental factors – friends, family, work – things around you.

Every one of these can lead to you giving up on the diet and/or the diet not working for you. Let's look at each of them in turn.

1. Doing the wrong diet.

The chances are that every diet you have tried so far has been trying to get you to eat less: calorie counting; very low-calorie liquid diets; high-street slimming clubs; any diet in a magazine etc. Even our governments tell us that we need to eat less and do more despite the fact that we have overwhelming evidence that this doesn't work long term. You may have tried low-carbohydrate diets, but you may not have addressed carbohydrate addiction and so these may seem to have failed for you. We'll come on to this in the food addiction section.

In essence, however, you have been trying to do the Minnesota Starvation Experiment. The 36 conscientious objectors couldn't stick to 1,600 calories a day and 45 minutes walking, despite being held captive. You are not going to be able to fare any better than they did. A calorie deficit diet inevitably makes you hungry and miserable. It would then only be natural to succumb to temptation whenever it appeared.

You have not failed; diets have failed you. This was not your fault. You just need to remember not to try to eat less (or do more) again and then this mistake won't be repeated.

2. Not getting expected results.
I see this one so often. Someone is really 'good'. They stick diligently to a diet for a few days, maybe a few weeks, but they don't get the expected results. The reaction all too often is: "Sod it. If I'm not going to get the results I expect, I may as well give up and eat what I want."

We've discussed the underlying problem behind this issue already – the calorie theory. Remember that woman in Chapter 2 who 'couldn't cope' with a weight loss of just two pounds per week when she had so much to lose? This is one of the reasons I attack the calorie theory so often and so vociferously. It is a lie. Not only is it a lie, it is a cruel lie. No one can say what your weight loss will be. It is individual and it depends on so many factors. Now that you know that it depends on one hormone – glucagon – to break down body fat, you can see weight loss in a very different light. Your role is to give glucagon every chance to break down body fat. You can enable this; you can't force it.

The first thing to rethink, therefore, is the expectation set unforgivably by the calorie myth. The weight loss for someone who moves from a low-calorie/high-carbohydrate diet to a real-food/managed-carbohydrate diet can be spectacular. I've seen people lose several pounds in the first few days. The weight loss thereafter is more likely to be erratic than steady – a pound here, two pounds there, a plateau, another pound – weight loss is variable; it's not formulaic.

I advise people to view weight loss as a 'chipping away' exercise. Lose a pound or two, maintain, lose another couple of pounds, maintain. Try to see the maintain/plateau periods as times when at least you are not gaining, which is what will happen if you really do say "sod it" and go back to eating what you like.

You must also remember that a pound lost by eating better (not less) need not go back on. You've seen the evidence in Chapter 2 for what happens with calorie deficit dieting – weight is lost in the short term, but then invariably regained and often with more on top. You are not going to make this mistake again. You are going to eat better, not less, and keep chipping away at your body fat.

As well as the 'chipping away' mentality, two further things can help with this common reason for giving up:

i) Consider not weighing yourself. If your inclination is to give up when the scales don't give you the 'reward' that you're looking for, then don't get on the scales. If weighing is more likely to demotivate you than to motivate you, then don't do it.

ii) Whatever you decide to do about weighing, do develop non-weight measures of success. Go back to the list in your notebook that you captured in Chapter 6 – where you were asked to write down everything troubling you right now, to establish a pain motivator. This could be: cravings, disturbed sleep, headaches, bloating, energy highs and lows, missing out on social events etc. As you eat better, make a note of non-weight things that you notice improving. Are you sleeping better? Is your skin clearer? Do you have more even energy throughout the day and fewer sugar highs and lows? Do you feel more inclined to go out and see friends?

Results are motivational. They do encourage us to keep going. Make sure that you have a number of measurable things to motivate you – not just the number on the scales (which can vary for all sorts of reasons anyway – water retention, time of the month, recent food intake and bowel movements etc).

The successful dieter is the one who can maintain commitment even when they don't feel that they are losing weight right now. These tips will help to lessen the expectation of the scales, but to win at weight loss, you need to be the person who doesn't give up. You may also like to ask yourself – where will giving up get me? What will that achieve? OK – so you can eat whatever you want now, today, but you know that you can't do this every day or you may become obese and type 2 diabetic in no time. You need to eat well for every aspect of your health – not just your weight – so the sooner you make this habit, the better.

3. Food addiction.

A number of things in this world baffle me. One of these is the fact that there is even debate as to whether or not food is addictive. Human beings have been put in MRI scanners and shown pictures of their favourite junk foods and their brains have responded in the same way as those of cocaine addicts. Yet there are people who deny that you can be addicted to food. If you personally have any doubt, make a note in your notebook of how you feel for the first few days when you start eating real food and only real food. I expect that you will get withdrawal symptoms from sugar, if not flour and other common substances.

In my book *Why do you overeat? When all you want is to be slim*, which was first published in 2004,[39] I presented the following four-stage process as a model for describing food addiction:

i) We have a craving for a particular food (or a number of foods). Let's use chocolate as an example.

ii) We develop increasing tolerance to chocolate, so that we need more and more chocolate to produce the same effects.

iii) We develop physical or psychological dependence. When we consume chocolate, we have an immediate sense of wellbeing (euphoria in the extreme). As the addiction worsens, we get to the stage where we need to eat chocolate, not just to feel good, but because we feel bad when we don't have it. Chocolate has become necessary to avoid unpleasant withdrawal symptoms.

iv) We suffer adverse effects from our addiction. With food addiction, these adverse effects can include: unbearable food cravings, weight gain, headaches, bloating, water retention, fatigue and so on. In extreme cases of food addiction, the adverse effects can include obesity, type 2 diabetes and possibly even heart disease. If food addiction had no adverse effects, we would just eat junk all day long. If we didn't feel terrible and gain weight, we would have no reason to confront our problem. However, we do suffer adverse effects and these effects get worse, not better. At some stage, the consequences of our addiction get so bad that we have to act. It's tough that we are usually at Stage 4 of the addiction model before we feel compelled to act.

This model can explain any addiction, whether it involves cigarettes, alcohol, drugs or gambling. We have an inclination towards placing a bet. We don't get the same high from one bet and so we find ourselves placing more bets and risking bigger amounts. We start to feel bad when we're not gambling and then we suffer the consequences. For some people, tragically, losing their house and family is the Stage 4 consequence that drives change.

In many ways, food is the worst addiction to have. We can avoid cigarettes. We can avoid alcohol. We can avoid betting shops and websites. We can't give up food. We need to eat. This is true, but we can give up certain foods and we need to abstain from the foods to which we are addicted.

I have written entire books about food addiction and the physical and psychological reasons why we crave food. Here is my five-day plan for a quick fix to tackle food addiction and cravings head on.

The five-day plan

The five-day plan avoids the most common sources of food intolerance in modern diets: sugar, wheat and milk. These are the substances most likely to be in anything that you are currently craving. Coming off the things that you crave is tough for the first few days – I won't claim otherwise. However, after five days (which is more than enough time for food to be digested by the body), your cravings are usually substantially reduced, enabling you to stick far more easily to real food as a long-term lifestyle choice.

The five-day plan follows the principles of Chapter 5 (the diet to lose weight) but it also avoids milk and cheese and it limits carbohydrate intake. This five-day plan is called Phase 1 of The Harcombe Diet and it consistently delivers quite spectacular weight loss. Use this any time you feel yourself becoming addicted to (craving) a certain food or foods. You can also use it any time you need a rapid weight loss fix.

The bottom line is that you can't be an addict in moderation. You can't overcome alcoholism by having a drink here and there. You can't give up smoking by just having a few. You need to stop eating whatever you feel addicted to. That is most likely to be processed food based around sugar and flour.

So, follow the diet in Chapter 5, which takes you back to the basics of unprocessed meat, fish, eggs, natural live yoghurt (avoid this if you know you are intolerant to dairy products) and vegetables (potatoes don't count as vegetables).

The five-day plan allows a small portion (50g dry weight/150g for vegetarians) of a 'safe' grain – not wheat, but brown rice, quinoa or porridge oats. Even fruit is avoided in the first five days, as fruit is essentially just sugar and you will find it easier to avoid sweet things if you avoid them entirely at the outset.

You can go back to fruit, cheese, baked potatoes and other grains after the five-day plan and even dark chocolate and red wine in time.

But, by choosing real food and choosing that real food for the nutrients it provides, you'll kick-start the good new habit of sticking mostly to the basics of meat and two veg. (Granny was right!)

THE FIVE-DAY PLAN – WHAT TO EAT

Any unprocessed meat (see list in Chapter 5)
Any unprocessed fish (see list in Chapter 5)
Eggs
Natural live yoghurt (if OK with dairy products)
50g (dry weight)/150g for vegetarians of brown rice, quinoa or porridge oats
Any vegetables (except potatoes)
Cook with butter or olive oil
Misc: tofu, olives, tomatoes, any herbs, spices & seasoning

4. 'Weakness' at the point of choice.

You know how this one works. You're doing well with your diet. You're feeling nicely committed to healthy eating and weight loss and then temptation appears in your path. Before you know what's happening, you're eating a piece of cake and then you feel that you've blown it, so you start eating all the things that you've been avoiding for a while and the ugly addiction monster rears its head again.

Some of this may be related to food addiction. However, I'll treat this as a separate one, as we have a plan to overcome food addiction. Let's assume that you weren't feeling addicted to cake; it was a genuine case of succumbing to temptation at the point of choice. If you have done this in the past, here's how to learn from that mistake so that it is not repeated:

i) Acknowledge that foods rich in the unnatural combination of fat and sugar are highly pleasurable. Giving in to that temptation is understandable – we just need to develop a strategy to resist it. What we are doing in that moment is 'choosing' immediate pleasure over the long-term (and far more satisfying) pleasure of being slim and healthy. However, I bet it didn't feel like a conscious choice, which brings us on to:

ii) Make a conscious choice. Never make an unconscious choice. Have you heard of that saying "a moment on the lips, a lifetime on the hips"? It's a great one for what's going on here. It really will only take you a couple of minutes to eat something that can undo your good intentions and efforts. It really isn't worth it. Consciously you know this. If you thought about what you're about to do, you could probably talk yourself out of it. So that's what you need to do.

iii) Use one of the habits from *The Seven Habits of Highly Effective People*.[40] The first habit in this brilliant book by Stephen Covey is often misunderstood. It is summarised as "Be proactive". This doesn't mean "go out and do something"– it means don't be reactive. Seeing a cake and eating it is being reactive. When the coffee shop assistant asks if you want anything with your coffee, ordering a muffin is being reactive. Walking into a petrol station intending to pay for your fuel and walking out with a confectionery bar is being reactive. Don't be reactive when it comes to food – ever – it won't end well.

You need to be highly conscious of every occasion of temptation until you become unconsciously competent. I haven't had a biscuit this century. There were days when I couldn't go an hour without a biscuit. If anyone offered me a biscuit now I would refuse on autopilot. It would be like being offered a cigarette. I wouldn't even think 'do I want a biscuit?' I would say no without even thinking about it.

You will get to that stage with whatever junk currently holds interest for you. It comes after a few weeks, not years. However, until you automatically say no, you need to consciously say no. Put nothing in your mouth without having made a conscious choice to do so.

Covey explains how we do this – by putting a space between an action and a reaction, so that we can choose our response thoughtfully. If you see the cake at work, pause, step away and ask yourself do you really want two minutes of flour and sugar diverting you from your SMART goal? Do you want the sugar high? Maybe. Do you want the inevitable crash that follows? Probably not. If you see the cake in a coffee shop or café, think of it like this: the shop assistant is trying to push drugs (sugar) on you because seven out of 10 purchases are made on impulse. Know this. Be angry about this. Vow not to be one of the people being made fat and sick to boost the profits of the junk-food industry.

You don't need to be as strong as you might think at the point of choice – you just need to be conscious.

There's one more issue to address to make sure that you have the tools to make this time different: what in your day-to-day environment might scupper your success?

5. Environmental factors – friends, family, work – everything around you.

I remember being at a conference when a young mother asked a question about noise pollution. She obviously lived in an incredibly noisy area and she described the effect that it was having on her and her family. Her ailments were real: zombie-like exhaustion, depression, anxiety and stress. The audience could feel her despair and pain. The presenter said that she needed to move and I thought: "That's not very helpful."

Then the mother continued to describe how awful her life was and the presenter continued to say that she needed to move. It wasn't long before I was siding with the presenter. She needed to move. Her life wasn't worth living. Yes, moving would be difficult. Yes, it would involve rethinking other fundamental aspects of her life – work, schools etc – but she might be able to minimise many of these. Maybe she could move away from the noise, but without having to change jobs/schools. Maybe she could rent the house out and rent somewhere else.

The presenter was trying to help with good and practical suggestions, but the mum could not get past her position that moving was not an option. She had created her own rock and hard place. Moving was unimaginable and living where she did was unimaginable. It made me realise that, if our goal is important and something is getting in the way of that goal, we need to move the obstacle.

It also made me realise that our preparedness to tackle obstacles, to accept change, may depend on how bad a place we are currently in. We may think that giving up the night out getting drunk is a step too far to achieve our goals. Getting some worrying medical results may change that.

Is there anything in your environment that is getting in the way of you being slim and healthy? Do your family insist on having junk in the house? Is work your downfall? The sandwich trolley? The office feeder? Being on the road as a salesperson?

Go back to your notebook and write down any such environmental challenges in your life. Then write down what you can do to overcome them...

161

How to overcome obstacles

My years working in HR taught me that there are only three responses to any situation:

1. Accept the situation
2. Change the situation
3. Walk away from the situation

This applies to every aspect of your environment that you identify as a potential obstacle to your progress. Back to the noise pollution, the young mum couldn't accept the situation; she couldn't change the situation, so she needed to physically remove herself from the situation. What can you accept? What can you change? What do you need to walk away from? Let's use the environmental challenges mentioned above as examples:

Obstacles	Overcoming them
Partner/family has junk in the house	Accept it: know that the junk is there and use it as an opportunity to be even stronger in your resolve.
	Change it: ask your partner to join you in your lifestyle change and/or to stop keeping junk in the house.
	Walk away (i.e. remove yourself from the risk): buy a safe and ask them to keep the junk there and never to tell you the code.

Obstacles	Overcoming them
There's a vending machine at work	Accept it: make sure that you're not hungry so that the temptation is massively reduced
	Change it: campaign to have it removed or to have healthy options added.
	Walk away: change your route so that you don't pass it. Don't carry money in your pocket or bag.
The sandwich trolley at work	Accept it: as above, don't be hungry. Enjoy feeling virtuous when you see others buying junk and you save your money.
	Change it: you could ask them to stock one healthy thing for you.
	Walk away: arrange meetings for the time the trolley arrives. Don't take money to work. Enlist a colleague to keep you strong.
A job on the road	Accept it: this is easier than it once was: real-food/low-carb has finally gone mainstream. High-street coffee chains now sell boiled egg and spinach boxes or fish salads. At motorway service stations you can buy main meals based on meat, fish, eggs, salads and veg.
	Change it: the more real food items you buy on the road, the more outlets will stock them.
	Walk away: be prepared. Take a tub of yoghurt or a lunch box out with you or have a big breakfast and get into the habit of skipping lunch.

And finally the 'feeder'

We need to talk about the 'feeder'. The feeder may be living with you or the feeder may be at work. In the next chapter we will look at the psychology of the feeder – perhaps it is the parenting style they have experienced that makes them do this. Until then, we don't need to know where the roots of their behaviour lie; we just need to make sure that they don't derail us.

If someone at home is not supporting you, that's OK – you can still take control of your own destiny and support yourself (get support from other family members, friends, online forums etc). However, if someone at home is actively trying to sabotage your good intentions, that's another matter and it needs to be resolved.

The most common reason for partner sabotage is that the partner fears change. They fear you changing. They fear you not feeling the same way about them if you do change. At the extreme, some partners fear that you will leave them if you feel attractive. You need to reassure them that you will feel better if you eat better. You will feel better if you look better. You are likely to be around for them longer and enjoying far better health if you are not suffering from obesity, type 2 diabetes or other debilitating conditions.

If your partner could benefit from eating better too, do everything you can to encourage them to join you. If they have a weight problem, they probably have an addiction and they will fear not being able to get their fix if they join you in a lifestyle change. Share this book with them, or your learnings from it, and explain that their addiction will only get worse, so the sooner they sort it the better.

The feeder at work can more easily be avoided. They generally mean well, although they are misguided in a world where two thirds of people are overweight. Like the sandwich trolley, if you know when the feeder brings in the junk – home-made cakes, biscuits, sweets etc – avoid being around at this time. Arrange a meeting… don't go to the kitchen if that's where the feeder leaves the junk that they have made (it's still junk – just home-made sugar/flour junk). We came up with some office feeder strategies in our Harcombe Diet online forum and our best three were:

i) Use humour: "Crikey – don't let me near that cake if you want anyone else to have some."

ii) Repeat the words "No, thank you" ad infinitum: "Would you like some cake?" "No, thank you." "Just a small slice?" "No, thank you." "Oh – go on – just try it." "No, thank you." "I made it specially." "No, thank you."

iii) Be blunt. With a particularly persistent drug pusher, you need to make them see what they are doing. Imagine that you were an ex-smoker and someone was trying to push a cigarette on you. Imagine that you were an alcoholic and someone was trying to make you drink. Share those examples with the sugar pusher. "If I were an alcoholic, you wouldn't dream of trying to get me to drink. Food has been my addiction in just the same way, so please don't try to push food on me."

In summary

People say "I've tried everything" and because nothing has worked, there is a dreadful sense of doom that nothing can work and that the distressing weight problem will never go away. Unless you have tried not trying to eat less, you haven't tried everything. Unless you have tried a lifestyle change, not a diet, you haven't tried everything. Unless you have tried real food with managed carbohydrate intake, you haven't tried everything. There are still things to try – don't give up. Or as Bill Clinton says, "never quit, never quit, never quit."

The lifestyle change proposed in this book will address the main reasons for previous 'failure'. You won't be 'going on a diet'. You will start something that you can maintain for life. You won't be trying to eat the foods that you crave in moderation. You are no more capable of doing that than an alcoholic is capable of having drink in moderation. You haven't failed; advice has failed you. Let's now take a look at just how deep rooted our relationship with food is.

9

How to understand and change your relationship with food

"You know what's healthier than kale? Having a good relationship with food."
Social media

I suspect that, for many people reading this book, the most significant relationship in their life is with food. That is terribly sad and we're going to change it. Food is just fuel and we need to see it as that – it's petrol for the car, it's water for the garden. It needs to stop being our best friend and our worst enemy alike.

The roots of our relationship with food

It is understandable that food takes too important a place in many lives because that's what happens from the moment we pop out into this world. We have the original bonding and nurturing relationship with Mum through breastfeeding.

At some stage we'll be moved on to infant formula – or baby milkshakes as Dr Robert Lustig calls them – or baby food, which can also be a concoction of sugar and starch. That starts our love of unnaturally sweet things.

Then the world of the child becomes one of 'treats' and reward. We fall over; we get a sweet to cheer us up. We celebrate a birthday with cake… Halloween with sweet 'treats'… Easter with chocolate eggs and hot cross buns… Before we can barely walk, we have established a strong connection between junk and feeling good. This did not happen by chance. It is in the interests of the junk-food industry that we develop an ingrained, subconscious love of their products for a lifetime.

Whenever there is a new childhood obesity initiative I get calls from various radio stations to do media interviews. They know that I will argue for greater restrictions on junk being advertised/given to children and that I will argue against sugar generally. The presenter will often play the devil's advocate and accuse me of being a killjoy, part of the nanny state – what's wrong with some sweets or crisps for goodness sake? I then list all the occasions when children are given junk: sugary cereal for breakfast; a biscuit or cereal bar mid-morning; school lunches are shocking arrays of pizza, chips, burgers, fish fingers, chicken nuggets – followed by a sugary pudding every day. Then there's the snack when the child gets home from school, then more sugar and starch for most dinners and then often milk and a biscuit before bed. And that's before we factor in birthdays, Halloween, Christmas, Easter, holidays, meals out and so on.

I am quite happy to be seen as a killjoy if it means speaking out about the current statistics: nearly a quarter of children in England are obese or overweight by the time they start primary school aged five, and this rises to one third by the time they leave aged 11.[41]

I also make the point – if you must give a child some junk food, please can you tell the child that it's junk food. Don't call it a treat. Don't let the child get to adulthood thinking that junk cheers them up, junk makes a bad day better, junk is fun, junk is a celebration, junk is a token of love. That adult will then have at least 18 years of indoctrination to overcome – often 50 or 60 such years – when they try to address their bad relationship with food and to lose weight.

I once met a TV producer, Sarah, who used to allow her seven-year-old boy "one bad thing a day". He could choose – a small bag of crisps, a small confectionery bar or a small fizzy drink. How long would it be before he asked: "Mummy, why do I have any bad things each day?"

If you are a parent reading this, it is never too late to change the message: junk is junk, it is not a treat. For those of you who have had the bad conditioning, you now have the tool to overcome this – the conscious incompetence model. Every time you find yourself thinking junk is good; junk is fun; junk will cheer me up, change the message: junk is junk; junk will make me fat; junk will give me a sugar crash and irritability and depression; junk will give me a puffy carb-face. Capture the worst ones that you can think of in your notebook.

The four pillars of childhood

During my HR training I came across a wonderful model called "The four pillars of childhood".[42] These are the four necessary conditions for a person's esteem to develop positively in the key formative years (generally seen as up to the age of five). The four pillars describe the things that parents and primary carers must do in those critical early years to ensure the optimal development of the child.

I added a Pillar 0 to the model, which I see as a precursor to the others being possible. Pillar 0 is the condition that our own parents and primary carers themselves have high self-esteem and good mental health during our formative years. It is very difficult for an adult to give a child the healthy nurturing that it needs, if the adult's own childhood was not a nurturing experience. Some unaware adults can even 'take out' their deficiencies on children in a particularly destructive way. Pillar 0 is quite a hurdle to overcome at the outset. It is little wonder that one in four people in the world will be affected by mental or psychiatric disorders at some point in their lives.[43]

In my experience, whenever adults were difficult in the workplace, invariably one or more essential childhood pillars was missing. These pillars are also a powerful base from which to understand any human behaviour – our adult relationship with food, for example.

Pillar 1. Unconditional love and positive reinforcement (from parents and primary carers in the formative years).

The child has to know that s/he is completely loved and valued, without conditions; otherwise a feeling of worthlessness can so easily develop. Conditional love occurs when a parent places a condition on their love for the child, e.g. "I don't love you when you're naughty." This implies that the child is only loved when they are 'good', whatever good means.

"Only children who eat their greens are allowed to have ice-cream." This directly links food to emotional situations at a formative age, and it sets conditions, such as I will only do nice things for you (give you ice-cream) if you do what I want (eat your greens). Such conditions are confusing for a child, and potentially destructive.

Pillar 2. Discipline.

All children need boundaries to go with this unconditional love. A dog cannot be content without knowing their place in 'the pack', as, in the absence of direction, they think that they are the master and stress about the responsibility that this involves. A child, similarly, needs to know what they can and can't do, or they get overloaded with decision making. They will push the boundaries – this is part of growing up – but the boundaries need to be there and they need to be reasonable and consistent. Having no boundaries can be as stressful as having too many. Unreasonable boundaries are harmful (e.g. children have to be out of sight when adults are around) and inconsistent boundaries mess with the young child's mind, as they are trying to get some sense of order in the world around them. A strict bed time of 7pm one night, then 10pm another, then 8pm another – without any logical reason for this – is the opposite of reassuring discipline.

Pillar 3. Encouragement and respect for our own personal development.
Acknowledgement that we are important is vital. We need to know that our opinions count; adults should not be dismissive. Sports coaches learn that you should deliver at least six or seven positive messages for every one corrective message. Even where the correction is helpful, e.g. "you need to commit earlier to the tackle", the sports leader needs half a dozen other "well dones" or "great jobs" to get the right balance of encouragement. We almost can't tell children too often how wonderful they are, how well they have just done, and so on, to cement this pillar of esteem.

Pillar 4. Self control – by this we mean 'control of the self' – feeling safe and having one's own space.

An infant or child exposed to serious neglect or harm, like abuse, hunger or cold, for example, will lose any sense of having control of their self. Abuse of a young child can take many forms and it is well documented that one of the worst kinds is neglect. This goes to the core of a person not being 'validated' and therefore not feeling entitled to be part of the world. In most circumstances, a child would obviously prefer i) positive attention and good parenting; but failing that they will take ii) negative attention and bad parenting (at least they have some attention). The absolute worst-case scenario is iii) no attention. I am fascinated by the parallels with animals and children – particularly dogs, a man's best friend. A dog would rather be beaten by its master (attention) than abandoned or ignored. Being ignored by the master is the dog's worst nightmare.

Pillar 4, control of the self, is about us feeling that we have control over our lives to the right extent at the right age. In writings about the four pillars, focus is often placed on the most extreme examples of abuse or neglect, but just as important is the point that general control must be given over to a child at the right age at the time. If your parents rarely let you decide basic things: what to wear; what to eat; when to eat; when to sleep; when to wake up; who to play with, and so on – and particularly if there is little evolution of these key decision-making milestones as you get older – you will not have adequate control of the self.

The four pillars and eating disorders

The four pillars (and 'ground zero') can provide such a useful model for individuals (and counsellors) to understand whether esteem issues need to be addressed and where the roots of these esteem issues may be. Thinking about our own pillars gives us as individuals a framework to understand our own esteem and sense of self. We can reflect on what was good about our upbringing and what was not so good. Most importantly, we can gain some invaluable insights into why we are the way we are and why we do certain things.

This is not about blame, or forgiveness, but about understanding what actually happened in our formative years and how this may be impacting on factors as diverse as performance, our drive to achieve, anxiety, depression, emotions and emotional eating in our lives today.

If we are lacking in any, or all, of these foundational pillars, our emotional development will have been impaired. It is then important to understand in what ways it has been impaired, so that we can make up for anything missing, as best as we are able to, as adults. Often, simply knowing what we lacked when younger and understanding why we are the way we are and why we do the

174

things we do, can help us to feel better about ourselves. It removes the mystery of things that we find ourselves doing, or having thoughts that we would rather not have. When we know why we are the way we are, we can start to be the person we want to be.

Discovering the four pillars was revolutionary in my understanding of myself and my relationship with food. As can so easily happen, my first calorie-controlled diet developed into anorexia. The pillars provide a comprehensive insight into this, which is particularly helpful as anorexia is the most difficult of eating disorders to understand.

Anorexia is not about food; anorexia is about low self-esteem and a need to control. Food just happens to be the weapon. Too little of Pillar 1 (unconditional love) and Pillar 3 (encouragement) can create a teenager with poor self-esteem. Too much of Pillar 2 (discipline) and insufficient Pillar 4 (allowing appropriate control of the self) can create a teenager desperate to regain control and a sense of self. That was me and my four pillars to a tee.

Anorexia helps to restore the self-esteem that the child lacked, as it provides an instantaneous way of making the individual feel good. The person with anorexia abstains from eating and they immediately feel virtuous and strong-willed. They get on the scales and they get the positive feedback (that they lacked from their elders) that they have 'done well'. This becomes a self-sustaining feedback loop in the short term, but a terribly destructive vicious cycle in the longer term.

Anorexia is also about control, and the teenager exerts it over one of the most basic needs – food. Young women, especially, assert themselves absolutely in an attempt to regain control of the self. Often well-behaved girls don't rebel, get expelled, take drugs or get pregnant – their statement of control is to take back ownership of the most basic need in life: food and drink.

The four pillars and parenting styles

I was invited to speak at the first low-carb international convention in South Africa in February 2015. It was an extraordinary experience – to be on the same platform as many of my own heroes such as Gary Taubes. I met someone there called Dr Robert Cywes and I'm ashamed to say that I misjudged him. I'm not a fan of bariatric surgery. (It spell-checks to barbaric surgery and that's probably appropriate!) Robert is a bariatric surgeon and I allowed this fact to prejudice my view of him. Robert does use bariatric surgery as a tool, but it's his tool of last resort and he uses it alongside treatment for food addiction. After spending 10 days together for the conference and in correspondence since, Robert has become my favourite expert on carbohydrate addiction in the world.

Robert introduced me to the work of Diana Baumrind, a development psychologist. In a ground-breaking 1967 article,[44] Baumrind identified three types of behaviour in pre-school children, which were strongly connected to three parenting styles. Baumrind called these parenting styles authoritative, authoritarian and permissive.

- AuthoritaTIVE parents ('firm, but fair') were described by Baumrind as: communicative, demanding, nurturing and controlling. I think that these are old-fashioned, 1960s words that could represent the four pillars well: love, discipline, encouragement and control (at an appropriate level for the child). The children of these parents were described as self reliant, self-controlled, explorative and content.
- AuthoritaRIAN parents ('disciplinarians') were non-communicative, demanding, non-nurturing and controlling. The children raised in this way exhibited signs of being discontented and distrustful, even at pre-school age. That sounds like too much of Pillar 2, insufficient Pillars 1 and 3 and inappropriate Pillar 4.
- Permissive parents were described by Baumrind as non-controlling. Their children were described as immature and dependent.

Maccoby and Martin developed Baumrind's ideas by distinguishing between permissive parents who are indulgent with their children and permissive parents who are uninvolved with their children.[45] This split permissive parenting into two variants, giving us four different parenting styles overall. I think that this is a really useful enhancement. The outcome for a child will be quite different depending on whether or not parents are indulgent and lenient, or indifferent and uninvolved.

Permissive and indulgent parenting would imply good Pillars 1 and 3 (love and encouragement), but poor Pillars 2 and 4 (discipline and control).

Indifferent and uninvolved parenting could be the worst outcome of all – none of the four pillars being present, as a foundation for personal development.

I've used Baumrind's observations and the Maccoby and Martin addition of a fourth parenting style to develop the following illustration.

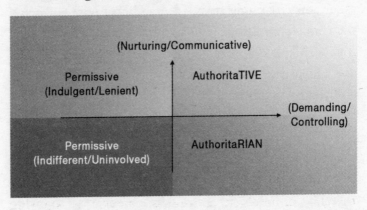

In Robert's experience of working almost exclusively with morbid obesity and the extremes of carbohydrate addiction, the people who end up in his clinic have come from either authoritaRIAN or permissive parents. The authoritaRIAN offspring set ridiculously high standards and then beat themselves up when they fail to meet them. This sense of failure erodes their self-esteem and they vow to achieve even tougher targets to regain their sense of control and self-worth. This group is most prone to all or nothing, black and white thinking, e.g. I've slipped up on my diet just now, so I'm going to give up today (and eat everything in sight) and then start again tomorrow. If this type can't be 'good', then they may as well blow the day completely.

The permissive group rarely invest effort in something worthwhile and seek the next easy 'high' instead. Their self-esteem is also low because they rarely put in the effort that achieves results and a sense of accomplishment. They probably haven't been encouraged to stretch themselves, as their parents weren't demanding in a positive way. This type tends to half-heartedly start a diet, if at all. They don't have the discipline (literally) to set a goal and work towards it.

Do you remember Dr Jen Unwin's questions in Chapter 7? What would you like to achieve and what are you prepared to do to achieve it? If you doubted your ability to commit to a goal and to achieve it, maybe you were the child of indulgent, permissive parents. Just knowing this may help you to realise that you can change your behaviour in the future. You can choose a different path knowing why you may have lacked resolve in the past.

The teenager with anorexia is most likely the child

of authoritaRIAN parents. The teenager with obesity is most likely the child of permissive parents. However, offspring of any parenting style can end up with a distressing weight problem and a destructive relationship with food.

We may, of course, have experienced a number of different parenting styles. Parents sometimes think it's a good idea (which it isn't) to play 'good cop/bad cop', where one is seen as loving (permissive indulgent) and the other is seen as strict (authoritaRIAN). Many parents do this without having made a conscious decision to do so. Marriages can break down and new parental figures can enter our lives and with them come different styles of interacting with us. Some parents change as we get older. When I reached my mid-teenage years my parents seemed to flick a switch from strong Pillar 4 (not giving me enough control of the self) and authoritaRIAN to being quite permissive and lenient. I look back now and see how I moved in parallel from anorexia to overeating. How useful that insight would have been at the time.

How do we change this?

This chapter has put our relationship with food at the forefront of our mind. We can clearly see the 'sweets are treats' indoctrination, to which we have been exposed. We have a model – the four pillars of childhood – to help us to understand our own earliest development and how this may have impacted on our sense of self and our behaviour. We have identified four parenting styles, at least one of which will resonate with our own upbringing. Those styles complement the pillars and show how the best parenting techniques deliver them. What do we do with all this?

One of my favourite books is *The Power of Now* by Eckhart Tolle.[46] Tolle firmly believes that we can develop considerably just by increasing our awareness. Tolle advises us to "become the watcher" – to observe what we are doing and to make conscious choices to stop doing unhelpful things. He's German so he tends to be pretty direct. There's a Q&A in the book and in it a woman who attended one of his talks asks a question about dropping unhealthy thoughts: "How can we drop negativity?" she asks. "How do you drop a piece of hot coal that you are holding in your hand?" Tolle replies: "By dropping it!"

Tolle's approach beautifully complements the four stages of competence model from Chapter 7. First we must catch ourselves doing something unhelpful – become the watcher – and move from unconscious competence to conscious competence.

If we don't know that we are doing something wrong, we can't change it. Tolle then encourages us to just drop it. Just stop doing it. The four stages approach is to consciously do it right and keep consciously doing it right until it is second nature (habit) to do it right. Doing it right/not doing it wrong are flip sides of the same coin.

It doesn't matter what we do – it matters that we start by observing anything that we are doing that is getting in the way of us achieving what we want to achieve. Then we can change things.

I'm now going to draw these concepts together to give some practical examples of unhelpful things that we do and how we can change our behaviour, using the parenting styles as a framework. Even if you have identified your own type strongly, do read the other bits as you may have some unhelpful behaviours from more than one type.

The child of authoritaRIAN parents

The child of authoritaRIAN ('disciplinarian') parents is prone to the following characteristics: perfectionism; having impossibly high standards; setting goals so tough that failure is almost inevitable; being an 'all or nothing' person; and thinking in black and white extremes. These characteristics can lead to the following behaviours with food:

- Setting unachievable diet goals, e.g. "I will lose 10lb by the weekend." "Today I will eat nothing but eggs and grapefruit."
- The 'all or nothing' attitude, e.g. "I was only going to eat fruit today, but I've just had some cereal so I've blown it. I'll start again tomorrow (and set an even

tougher target in punishment)". "I'm out on Saturday, so I can't do that five-day plan, so I'll just eat what I want this week and then be super strict next week."

Do these sound familiar? You may have an authoritaRIAN background if they do. Now that you can see where the roots of this behaviour lie, you can start to see the way out.

i) First, you need to stop setting such demanding and impossible goals – in all walks of your life possibly – but certainly in the arena of food. Think about your best friend and imagine giving them the goal "eat nothing but fruit today" – would you say such a thing? You need to start treating yourself with the love and care that you lacked as a child. You need to give yourself some of that nurturing that you missed out on. No more impossible goals for you – liberate yourself from your own tyranny.

ii) Second, you need to embrace shades of grey. Not necessarily 50! But certainly more than you probably do now. Seeing things in black and white is child-like. It is a sign of being grown up that you can see shades of grey. A young teenager might only see one view on fox hunting, for example. A grown-up can see different views, even if they don't agree with them. You need to let go of the black and white, good and bad world and learn to live with the shades of grey. The black and white response to having cereal, when you vowed only to have fruit, is that the day can now only be bad, so it may as well be very bad and then you can eat whatever you want. The grey response is: "It's only a bit of cereal. I shouldn't have set such a tough target. I won't do it again. I haven't ruined anything. I'll stop the fruit fad and have a healthy dinner."

iii) Finally, vow to learn from every slip. When there is no longer black and white, good and bad, there is also no success and failure and what we really want to end is any sense of failure. It is horrible to make yourself constantly feel like a failure. It's cruel. Back to your best friend – you wouldn't do this to them. Please stop doing it to yourself.

So the 'F' word, for failure, is banished from the dictionary. There are only opportunities to learn. If anything goes wrong, learn from it. What could you have done differently? Did you set an impossible goal? Did you flip into that "I've blown it" mentality all too easily? Did you just get hungry? What can you do differently next time so that it doesn't happen again?

The child of permissive parents

The child of indulgent/lenient permissive parents is prone to the following characteristics: feeling directionless; having low respect for authority; expecting demands to be met; getting things without effort; unreasonableness; a sense of entitlement. Veruca Salt in Roald Dahl's *Charlie and the Chocolate Factory* is the extreme characterisation of this type, but the child of indulgent/lenient parents will have some similarities – they may not have been stretched, may not have been encouraged to set and achieve goals, may have been spoiled (highly likely with junk food, as well as other presents). You can see how this parenting style, while intended to be kind, is anything but.

The child of indifferent/uninvolved permissive parents is the most likely to rebel, not least to try to get the attention that has been so lacking. This child will feel directionless and lack respect for authority, but they will also have a strong will and sense of independence, having been used to looking after themselves because no one else does.

Permissive parents, thankfully, are more likely to be indulgent/lenient than indifferent/uninvolved. The parents of my generation tended to be the authoritaRIAN types. And a number of my peers reacted to the discipline and over-control of their parents by vowing to be very different. However, in their own parenting, many have swung the other way and given too little discipline and too few boundaries. This fails the Pillar 2 need in children. They have also given children too much control of the self too young (Pillar 4) and this is harmful, albeit entirely well intentioned.

There are reasons why parents should make many decisions for a child. It is too stressful for a child to have to make too many decisions. The parent should decide what the child wears, what they eat, which shoes to put on when they go out, when they go to bed etc. These are not decisions that a child needs, or wants, to make. Obviously, the number of decisions made by the parent should decline over time – that's Pillar 4 – but young children need parenting. Asking five-year-olds what they want for tea or eight-year-olds when they want to go to bed is not appropriate. The answers will be "sweets" and "late".

If you have been indulged as a child, you will find it difficult to stick to 'a diet'. You will have a stronger sense of deprivation than others. You will have developed a stronger sense of 'junk is a treat' than the average person. Food is likely to mean the same as 'feeling loved' to you. You are prone, therefore, to repeating this pattern of behaviour with your partners, friends, family and children. You may be the inadvertent 'office feeder' – the person who thinks that they are being caring and kind taking cake in for the office to share.

If this resonates with you, I sincerely hope that the Eckhart Tolle principle of "becoming the watcher" will help enormously. Just knowing why you find it difficult to stick to a healthy eating pattern can help you to overcome this hurdle. Shine the light on what has happened – you have been overindulged. That wasn't your fault. It doesn't have to have been anyone's fault; it is what it is. You can now use this enlightenment to understand why you have not done well before and how you can do well now. You're grown up now. You know that you can't have your cake and be slim. You know that it will take some effort to achieve your goal of healthy eating. You're not very experienced in goal setting and achieving, but all that is in the past. The enlightened you can achieve whatever you put your mind to.

Reflection

Take some time to think about the many concepts and suggestions in this chapter. Reflect on your own childhood – maybe even with childhood friends or siblings – and understand which pillars were strong and which were lacking. Make a note of observations in your notebook. Particularly note how maybe too little unconditional love and too much discipline may have affected you. Has a lack of encouragement and too much control given you a bad relationship with food, even if not fullblown anorexia? Have you been spoiled with food as love in a way that has been unhelpful for your eating patterns?

To reiterate, this is not about blame in any way. Our own parents suffered adversity in many ways that don't happen today (world war, inequalities, intolerance of diversity etc). Maybe that's why I thought to add Pillar 0. Many of our parents lacked stability in the parenting they themselves received, and certainly didn't have perfect pillars in their lives. This is about understanding how less than optimal development can be continued through generations and how it then impacts our lives.

Both my parents came from poor backgrounds and so they felt guilty about wasting any food. My mother spent much of her life dieting on the one hand and finishing off anything that my brother or I left on the other – unhelpful beliefs and practices. I know a woman who felt great pressure from her very slim and disciplined mother to be equally slim and disciplined (too much Pillar 2). She was angry at this pressure. She wanted to stick two fingers up to this pressure. So she did. She achieved the goal of showing her anger by becoming obese and upsetting her mother. Talk about cutting one's nose off to spite one's face.

It is understandable how food has assumed so much prominence in most of our lives. This chapter explains how our upbringing and the food environment made this so. There is another reason why food has taken on a role beyond that which is healthy or useful. Food is the most acceptable and accessible drug. We can't drop the children at the school gate when we are drunk or high, but we can drop them off having just had a carb binge, and being every bit as 'drugged'.

Food is the omnipresent, affordable and acceptable drug. We can buy it in every outlet we walk into from a petrol station to a theatre. It has cheered us up from the first time we fell over. It has been our crutch ever since. Only it's a crutch that doesn't work. It momentarily distracts us from an emotional pain that we are trying to numb, but it doesn't deal with that pain and it has serious long-term consequences.

Someone is nasty to us and our well-honed instinct is to reach for junk to cheer us up. The upset hasn't been dealt with. The mean boss is still mean, or the unruly teenager is still unruly. This is no way in which to live life. We need to allow ourselves to experience emotions and not look to a drug to blot them out. The more we experience and deal properly with emotions, the more we will grow and develop as a person and the more we will be able to cope with emotions in the future. We can, in parallel, develop non-drug support mechanisms, but these should never be used to avoid situations. They should be used as genuine rewards when we handle something difficult.

For example, if an attack on social media would previously have had you reaching for the biscuit packet, use the next attack as a learning opportunity. What could you have done differently to avoid the attack? Do you enjoy fights? If not, don't pick them! If the attack was unjustified (and most are) don't let a troll derail you. Allow yourself to feel the emotion of being upset without reaching for a carb crutch.

Develop a means of preserving your sense of self without resorting to drugs. The best advice I ever received was from a teacher: "Only care about the opinions of those people whom you care about." Do you care what this troll thinks? No – then block/mute said troll and do not give them one second more of your precious time.

If your children say something hurtful, you do care about their opinion, but you also know that children are temperamental, volatile and lack the ability to express feelings in a sensitive way. Again – don't reach for the chocolate crutch – know that the moment will pass and live with the momentary upset without spoiling your long-term health.

Every time you feel emotional pain and refrain from reaching for the carb crutch, reward yourself in a non-food way. Put some money in a jar and buy something just for you when it reaches a certain amount. Be proud of yourself every time you break that bad lifelong habit of trying to block out pain. Be super proud of yourself when you deal with a difficult situation by finding the right words to have a difficult conversation – not by avoiding the conversation and having a binge instead.

Every day we have opportunities in life to grow and develop as a human being. Until now we may have missed many of them. That's now part of our past. Going forward we will have a different relationship with food

– a healthy relationship with food. Food will be fuel. It won't be a means for blocking out the world. Food will no longer be our best friend – it never was, to be honest – but it will never again be our worst enemy either.

10
Your 10-step plan for success

"The definition of insanity is doing the same thing over and over again, but expecting different results."

Narcotics Anonymous (1981)
(Often wrongly attributed to Albert Einstein)

This book is about losing weight and keeping it off for good. This chapter is the summary of everything we've covered. It's the one to reread any time you need a refresher course of what we've been through. The 10-step plan is summarised as follows:

Knowledge
Step 1. Know what doesn't work.
Step 2. Know what does work.

Values, goals and beliefs
Step 3. Accept that only you can do this.
Step 4. Understand your why (and what you're prepared to do to achieve it).

Step 5. Set SMART goals (Specific, Measurable, Achievable, Realistic and Timebound).

Step 6. Understand your beliefs – especially your limiting beliefs.

Tools

Step 7. Understand your relationship with food.

Step 8. Use tools to change your behaviour.

Act

Step 9. Eat naturally and move naturally.

Step 10. Just do it! One last time…

Knowledge

Step 1. Know what doesn't work.

Counting calories doesn't work. Trying to eat less doesn't work. Trying to do more doesn't work.

Chapter 1 shattered the myth that "To lose 1lb of fat you need to create a deficit of 3,500 calories." The powers-that-be know not from whence that myth came and they cannot prove it.

Chapter 2 documented the most important studies, from the past 100 years, which have shown that low-calorie diets don't work. Remember Sam, from the Minnesota Starvation Experiment, who was so desperate with hunger, he chopped his fingers off? He didn't even know if it was deliberate or delusional.

That seminal study, from 70 years ago, taught us four vital things:

i) Hunger is comparable with war in terms of the devastating effect it has on people.
ii) Weight loss on dramatically restricted calorie regimes is a fraction of the amount predicted.
iii) The less you eat, the less you must continue to eat to have any chance of losing more weight and weight loss will stop, at some point, whether you like it or not.
iv) The body will do whatever it takes to reverse the effects of starvation/dieting.

Chapter 3 explained why eating less and/or doing more doesn't work:

We can't sustain a calorie deficit.
We can't sustain a calorie deficit because trying to eat less makes us want to eat more and do less and trying to do more makes us want to eat more and do less. We are hard-wired to eat more and do less. We can't change that hard-wiring. We need to start working with our bodies – no more fighting the entire history of evolution.

Even if we could sustain a calorie deficit, the body adjusts.
Even if, in the short-term, we could sustain a calorie

deficit, the body eventually adjusts. There are nine systems in the human body – all of which can and do adjust. If we put less fuel in, the body does less – it doesn't just give up body fat. That's one of the last things that it wants to do, as body fat has been our survival blanket through times long before supermarkets existed.

Trying to eat less/do more makes us eat the wrong things and in the wrong way.
The mere act of trying to eat less drives bad food choices. We graze, to make us feel less deprived. We try to get the biggest bang for our calorie buck, to make us feel less deprived. This leads us to high-carbohydrate, low-fat foods, drip-fed throughout the day. This turns out to be the worst possible thing to do to lose weight.

Step 2. Know what does work.
Weight loss is the act of breaking down body fat. The hormone in the body that does this for us is called glucagon. Glucagon needs us to meet four conditions to be able to break down body fat:

i)   We must not have glucose available as fuel.
ii) We must not have insulin present.
iii) We need to do things that enable glucagon to be called upon;
iv) And not do things that inhibit the operation of glucagon.

That's the knowledge that we need to understand how to lose weight. Step 10 summarises the perfect healthy eating and movement plan to achieve these conditions.

Values, goals and beliefs

Step 3. Accept that only you can do this.
Once you have the requisite knowledge, the acceptance that you are the only person who can achieve your goal is the most vital next step. Take all the tips and inspiration that you need, but then accept that you – and only you – are the person who can achieve what you want.

You really can do this. Do you know the most common thing that people say when they lose a large amount of weight? "If I can do this, anyone can." That's because they had such low regard for their own ability to lose that weight. They think that everyone else in the world has more willpower and commitment than they do. Even if you are that person – the one who thinks that you have the lowest chance of achieving anything – you can be that same person saying: "If I can do this, anyone can."

Step 4. Understand your why (and what you're prepared to do to achieve it).
You've learned that there are only two motivators of change: pain and pleasure. You've learned that pain is the

greater motivator of the two. Is there a pain motivator that you can harness? The pain motivator may involve others – for example, concern that you may not be around for grandchildren. Many people with weight problems are the carers and feelers in this world and a goal that involves others may inspire you.

If not a pain motivator, is there a pleasure motivator that you can strongly visualise and connect with? We know that people want to be slim more than anything – the Florida study in the introduction showed that. You'd probably choose being slim for life over winning the lottery, so be bold in what you're prepared to do to achieve this.

If permissive parenting has knocked your confidence in achieving goals, shine the light on that limiting belief and change it.

Step 5. Set SMART goals (Specific, Measurable, Achievable, Realistic and Timebound).

Make your goal SMART. Because it's specific, measurable and timebound, you will be able to monitor your progress towards it. Because it's achievable and realistic, you will be able to get to the end you have in mind. Because it's written down in your notebook, you will be able to refer to it often.

Stick a copy on the fridge. Keep a copy in your purse or wallet. Maybe even make it your screensaver, so that you see it every time you look at your phone or PC. If you know where you're going, you're far more likely to get there.

Step 6. Understand your beliefs – especially your limiting beliefs.

Your notebook should be full of insights into what has stopped you achieving your goal in the past. It is likely to have been just the wrong dietary advice – trying to do the Minnesota Starvation Experiment for yourself. The chances are that along the way you have lost faith in yourself. You can change this. Indeed, only you can change this. There are some tools that can help…

Tools

Step 7. Understand your relationship with food.

Which ingrained messages from childhood are hampering your progress? Do you still think that sweets are treats? Have you always thought this? Which emotions do you associate with food? How can you generate or deal with those emotions in non-food ways? Be prepared for a period of rawness in emotions when you don't turn to food as a crutch. Be proud of every step you take when you handle emotions as they should be dealt with – with interpersonal skills and not food.

How were your childhood pillars? How much of the following did you have from your parents and primary carers in your formative years?

Pillar 1. Unconditional love and positive reinforcement.

Pillar 2. Discipline.

Pillar 3. Encouragement and respect for your personal development.

Pillar 4. Allowing you appropriate control of yourself.

And remember that one extra pillar to think about: did your parents and primary carers have their own necessary self-esteem and good mental health to be able to do the best for you?

The observations related to these issues will fit strongly with an overall parenting style. Were you fortunate to have 'firm but fair' authoritaTIVE parents? Or did you have more authoritaRIAN parents, 'disciplinarians' as we could call them? If your parents were more permissive, were they indulgent and lenient, or – let's hope not – indifferent and uninvolved?

Do you identify with the all-or-nothing, black and white thinking that is common with the children of disciplinarians, making you prone to set yourself brutal goals? Maybe permissive parenting has left you feeling less able to set goals, as everything was handed to you on a plate.

We can't change things unless we know that they need to change. This brings us nicely to…

Step 8. Use tools to change your behaviour.

- *The Power of Now.* Start by "becoming the watcher", as Eckhart Tolle advised. Observe your mind scripts – the mini plays that you put on in your head. Observe the messages that you give yourself by the minute, the hour and the day. You communicate more with yourself than with any other person. Which good and encouraging messages are you sending (that you can do more of)? Which unhelpful and critical messages are you sending (that you need to drop like a hot coal)?

- *The four stages of competence model.* This is your go-to tool to change any aspect of your thinking and/or behaviour that is getting in the way of you achieving your goal. An unhelpful mind script, a bad habit, a destructive action... Becoming the watcher will help you to spot it and in doing so you move from unconscious to conscious incompetence. Then you work on doing the right thing until you are consciously competent and it becomes second nature.

- *Reflection.* We have undertaken a number of reflection exercises in our notebooks – an excellent practice to make routine. As we are settling down at night, my husband and I will often ask each other: "What was the highlight of your day?" This sends us to sleep with a positive thought in mind.

You may like to reflect each Sunday night or Monday morning about how things have gone for you over the past week. Always start with positives – at least three; only when you have these written down are you allowed to think of what could have gone better. Notice that we don't call these negatives – they are always opportunities to learn. As you do this more and more often, you will learn more and more about yourself. All of this understanding will help you to achieve your goal.

Act

Step 9. Eat naturally and move naturally.
Adopt the following five principles and make them the way that you do things from now on:

Principle 1. Eat real food.
The essentials in a real-food diet are: meat, eggs and dairy foods – ideally from pasture-living animals; fish, vegetables and fruits – ideally those in season; beans and pulses, and non-wheat wholegrains, such as brown rice and oats.

Principle 2. Choose whatever real food you eat for the nutrients it provides.
When we factor in the essential nutrients – the complete protein, essential fats, vitamins and minerals that we must consume to survive and thrive – we will nat-

urally prioritise foods of animal origin (meat, fish, eggs and dairy) and green leafy vegetables, as these are the most nutrient-dense foods. This will naturally manage carbohydrate intake because meat and fish contain no carbohydrate (with the exception of glycogen in liver); eggs contain barely a trace and dairy products no more than 10%. Non-starchy vegetables are also naturally low in carbohydrate.

If you do want to choose carbohydrate meals from time to time, adopt the approach outlined in Chapter 5, avoiding combining them with the staples of fat meals – meat, fish, eggs and dairy products. The classic British meals, such as beef and Yorkshire pudding, cheese and bread 'Ploughmans' and fish and chips, are all wonderfully fattening.

Principle 3. Eat a maximum of three times a day.
Remember 'what does work' – enabling glucagon – and visualise flicking the fat-burning switch off every time you eat. Minimise the number of eating occasions each day to allow the maximum time possible burning fat.

Principle 4. Manage alcohol intake to enable fat burning.
The alcohol choice is yours – how much and how often. You know that you will inhibit the operation of glucagon for a period of time after drinking alcohol. Alcohol is one of life's pleasures and part of many social activities. You can decide when to enjoy a glass of wine or champagne

(ideally not beer or spirits and sugary mixers) armed with knowledge. You can also be prepared for the blood glucose dip that will follow alcohol consumption. The "4g of sugar in the blood stream" fact can be used to eat just the right amount of food to get your blood glucose back into the normal range. You will need one square of very dark chocolate or one bite of a piece of fruit. You won't need a kebab and pitta bread!

Principle 5. Do what we're designed to do: walk, talk, dance, sing, cook, clean and tend the land.

The good news is – you don't need to go to the gym to lose weight. You don't need to go jogging or sign up for the amateur Tour de France. Indeed, exercise can be unhelpful at times when you're trying to slim – as Gary Taubes so beautifully put it, it's how we work up an appetite.

Hopefully it will also be good news to know that you should find something that you do enjoy and do it as often as you can. Walking is the single best activity that you should do – as much as suits your lifestyle every day. Learn to dance? Become a street litter picking champion? Join a choir? This is your chance to do something active, natural and fun.

Step 10. Just do it! One last time...

We opened with Oprah's heartfelt words about her own struggle with her weight. All she needed to do was lose weight once and keep it off. Oprah went wrong when she started calorie-counting, lost weight, regained it and more. Then she did another calorie-controlled diet, lost weight, regained it and more. And another, and another…

The definition of insanity is doing the same thing over and over again, but expecting different results. To this extent, Oprah has been insane over her four decades of dieting. She consolidated this insanity in October 2015 by buying a stake in Weight Watchers®. The fact that one of the most brilliant women in the world can continue to make the same mistake just shows how powerful the calorie-counting belief is.

The Diet Fix

We almost called this the "Don't Diet!" book, but that would be to miss the point that a diet is not all about restricting food consumption; it is simply the term used to define 'the kind of food that a person habitually eats'. This book is about fixing your diet, so that you don't do what you might think of as 'going on a diet', i.e. eating less.

From now on, your focus will be on eating better, not eating less. Your eating philosophy will be about nourishment, not deprivation. We now know that to lose weight, we must change our lifestyle, not go on a diet – certainly not a calorie-controlled diet. We must make healthy eating, not starvation, our way of life.

Would you like some good news? When you follow the five principles in "Eat naturally and move naturally", you don't just lose weight; you start to feel great. People report sleeping better at night and having far more energy during the day. Daily energy is also typically more even – the sugar highs and crashes are a thing of the past. You may find that your skin is glowing and your hair is shiny – benefiting from the vitamins and minerals that you're consuming. Headaches tend to reduce, or disappear. Bloating, constipation and other gastrointestinal problems might no longer trouble you. One of the most frequent comments I hear from people who embrace real food is: "I started this to lose weight; I'm sticking with it because I feel so good!"

Here's some more good news: the longer that you do this for, the easier it becomes. The longer you avoid junk, the easier it becomes to avoid junk. You may feel that you're in a vicious cycle of eating bad food at the moment, feeling bad, reaching for more bad food, feeling even worse and so on. You can break into a virtuous cycle just as quickly. After a few days, not even weeks, you should feel cravings subside substantially and you will start to see some immediate health and weight benefits.

And some more good news: you will feel better about yourself for adopting "The Diet Fix". If you put junk into your body, you are treating yourself as if you were worthless – like a dustbin. If you put nutritious ingredients into your body, you are treating yourself with the care that you deserve. You may have started this book not feeling that you deserve to be slim, healthy and the best you that you can be. That's why we've looked so much at our relationship with food and our beliefs, where these have come from and how we can change them. You absolutely do deserve to be the best you that you can be and you are the person to make it happen...

Remember that fabulous Barack Obama quotation? *"Change will not come if we wait for some other person or some other time. We are the ones we've been waiting for. We are the change that we seek."*

Remember that we can do anything we set our minds to. Know this and be the person you so desperately want to be. I seem to remember that the first black president of the United States said something else that reflected the immensity of his own personal achievement: *"Yes, we can!"*

Over to you now. You can do it. One last time. You really can!

Acknowledgements

First, I would like to thank all the members of The Harcombe Diet club – Anne, Bethan, Carol, Christelle, Christine, Jen, John, Jules, Linda, Mat, Rosemary, Sistercas, Tracy and Weebear – for so kindly and openly sharing their personal stories about what finally motivated them to change. Their insights will inspire others who just need that "enough is enough" moment to make this their "one last time."

I would like to thank Rebecca Nicolson and Aurea Carpenter from Short Books for getting in touch to see if we could work together on a book. It has been the most delightful and stress-free experience and we are all thrilled with the result.

Last and never least I would like to thank my husband, my rock, my best friend, my coach and my chef: Andy. Most people wonder how a married couple can ever work together – we wonder why we didn't do it sooner!

References

1 Helen Fielding. Bridget Jones's Diary. First published by Picador, an imprint of Pan Macmillan (1996).

2 http://www.oprah.com/omagazine/what-i-know-for-sure-weight

3 Interview with Oprah Winfrey. People section. Arizona Republic. p315 (7th December 1986). https://www.newspapers.com/newspage/120303990/

4 E. Fothergill et al. "Persistent metabolic adaptation 6 years after 'The Biggest Loser' competition." Obesity (2016).

5 Gina Kolata. "The Science of Fat: After 'The Biggest Loser', Their Bodies Fought to Regain Weight." The New York Times (2nd May 2016). https://www.nytimes.com/2016/05/02/health/biggest-loser-weight-loss.html

6 Colleen S.W. Rand and Alex M. C. Macgregor. "Successful weight loss following obesity surgery and the perceived liability of morbid obesity". International Journal of Obesity (1991).

7 British Dietetic Association Leaflet. Want to Lose Weight and keep it off?

8 Lulu Hunt Peters. Diet and Health (with key to the calories). Published by The Reilly and Lee Company, Chicago (1918).

9 T.R. Van Dellen. "How to keep well." Chicago Daily Tribune (15th September 1959).

10 M.E.J. Lean, W.S. Leslie, A.C. Barnes, et al. "Primary care-led weight management for remission of type 2 diabetes (DiRECT): an open-label, cluster-randomised trial." The Lancet (2017).

11 A. Stunkard and M. McLaren-Hume, "The results of treatment for obesity: a review of the literature and report of a series." Archives of Internal Medicine (1959).

12 Ancel Keys. The Biology of Human Starvation. Published by

Minnesota University Press (1950). All details in this chapter about the experiment come from this publication.

13 Francis G. Benedict. Human vitality and efficiency under prolonged restricted diet. Carnegie Institution of Washington (1919).

14 Stunkard and McLaren-Hume, op. cit.

15 M.J. Franz et al. "Weight-loss outcomes: a systematic review and meta-analysis of weight-loss clinical trials with a minimum 1-year follow-up." Journal of the American Dietetic Association (2007).

16 E.C. Weis et al. "Weight-control practices among USA adults 2001-2002." American Journal of Preventative Medicine (2006).

17 C.D. Gardner et al. "Effect of low-fat vs low-carbohydrate diet on 12-month weight loss in overweight adults and the association with genotype pattern or insulin secretion: The diet fits randomized clinical trial." Journal of the American Medical Association (2018).

18 A. Fildes et al. "Probability of an Obese Person Attaining Normal Body Weight: Cohort Study Using Electronic Health Records." American Journal of Public Health (2015).

19 Gary Taubes. Why we get fat. Published by Random House (2011).

20 http://www.earlybirddiabetes.org/index.php

21 Katie M. Mallam et al. "Contribution of timetabled physical education to total physical activity in primary school children: cross sectional study." British Medical Journal (2003).

22 F.G. Benedict, J.A. Harris. "A Biometric Study of Basal Metabolism in Man." The Carnegie Institution of Washington (1919).

23 http://www.dailymail.co.uk/femail/article-2007073/Marathon-runner-Paula-Radcliffe-sets-winning-example.html (23rd June 2011).

24 L. Tappy. "Thermic effect of food and sympathetic nervous sys-

tem activity in humans." Reproduction Nutrition Development (1996).

25 J. Levine. "Nonexercise activity thermogenesis (NEAT): environment and biology." American Journal of Physiology – Endocrinol Metabolism (2004).

26 M.E.J. Lean et al., op. cit.

27 National Institute for Clinical Excellence. "Guidance on the prevention, identification, assessment and management of overweight and obesity in adults and children." Clinical Guidelines 43. Obesity (2006).

28 Melvin J. Konner. The Tangled Wing: Biological Constraints on the Human Spirit. 2nd edition Published by Times Books (2002).

29 Jeff Volek and Stephen Phinney. The Art and Science of Low Carbohydrate Living: An Expert Guide to Making the Life-Saving Benefits of Carbohydrate Restriction Sustainable and Enjoyable. Published by Beyond Obesity LLC (2011).

30 Zoë Harcombe. The Obesity Epidemic: What caused it? How can we stop it? Published by Columbus Publishing (2010).

31 Amrita Misha and Marina Basina. "Why doesn't glucagon work with alcohol?" (https://beyondtype1.org/why-doesnt-glucagon-work-with-alcohol/)

32 David Gillespie. Toxic oil: Why vegetable oil will kill you and how to save yourself. Published by Penguin (2013).

33 D.L. Swagerty et al. "Lactose intolerance." American Family Physicians, 65(2), 1845-1850. (2002). http://www.ncbi.nlm.nih.gov/pubmed/12018807

34 https://www.statisticbrain.com/new-years-resolution-statistics/

35 P. Elwood et al. "Healthy Lifestyles Reduce the Incidence of Chronic Diseases and Dementia: Evidence from the Caerphilly Cohort Study." Plos One (2013).

36 Y. Li, A. Pan et al. "Impact of Healthy Lifestyle Factors on Life

Expectancies in the US Population." Circulation (2018).

37 Jen Whitington. Fixing Dad: How To Save Someone You Love. Published by Short Books (2016).

38 http://www.wordsfitlyspoken.org/gospel_guardian/v20/v20n41p1-3a.html

39 Zoë Harcombe. Why do we overeat? When all we want is to be slim. Published by Columbus Publishing (2013).

40 Stephen Covey. The Seven Habits of Highly Effective People. Published by Free Press (1989).

41 NHS Digital. "National Child Measurement Programme 2016/17." (2017).

42 Maggie Gall. Child-Centered Attachment Therapy: The CcAT Programme (UK Council for Psycho-therapy). Published by Routledge (2009).

43 http://www.who.int/whr/2001/media_centre/press_release/en/

44 D. Baumrind "Child care practices anteceding three patterns of preschool behavior." Genetic Psychology Monographs (1967).

45 E.E. Maccoby and J.A. Martin. "Socialization in the context of the family: Parent–child interaction." P.H. Mussen, editor. Handbook of Child Psychology. Published by John Wiley (1983).

46 Eckhart Tolle. The Power of Now. Published by Yellow Kite (2001).

Index

215

Dr Zoë Harcombe is a Cambridge University graduate with a BA and MA in economics/maths. She enjoyed a successful career in global blue chip organisations before leaving corporate life to pursue her passion – diet and health. Zoë gained her PhD in public health nutrition in 2016 and has published several academic papers challenging accepted public health dietary advice. She was an independent board member for Cardiff Metropolitan University between 2006 and 2012 and an independent board member for the Welsh National Health Service between 2009 and 2012. She has published several books on diet and health, including *Stop Counting Calories & Start Losing Weight* (2008), *The Obesity Epidemic* (2010) and *The Harcombe Diet: Three Step Plan* (2013). Zoë has appeared regularly on radio and TV, featuring on Sky News, *Steve Wright in the Afternoon*, Radio 4's *The Food Programme*, ITV *Tonight* and BBC *Newsnight*, as well as Fox News in the US. She has also written for numerous magazines and most national newspapers, along with writing her diet and nutrition blog, zoeharcombe.com. Zoë lives with her husband and rescue animals in the Welsh countryside surrounded by food, a.k.a. sheep, hens and cows.